Beatles at the movies

scenes from a career

Paul McCartney John Lennon

George Harrison Ringo Starr

Beatles at the movies
scenes from a career

Roy Carr

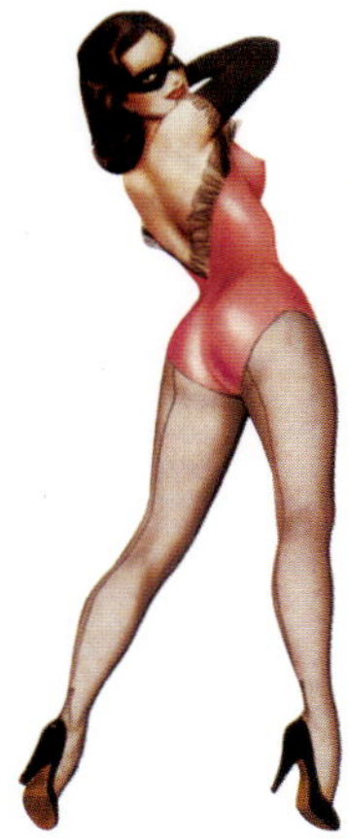

PHOTOGRAPHIC CREDITS

© HULTON DEUTSCH

© THE KOBAL COLLECTION

© LONDON FEATURES INTERNATIONAL LTD

© MIRROR SYNDICATION INTERNATIONAL LTD

© PICTORIAL PRESS

© POPPERFOTO

© RANGE PICTURES LTD

© REDFERNS

© REX PICTURES

© UFO MUSIC LTD

UFO Music Ltd 18 Hanway Street London W1P 9DD England
Telephone: 0171 636 1281 Fax: 0171 636 0738

First published in Great Britain 1996
UFO Music Ltd 18 Hanway Street
London W1P 9DD

The author and publishers have made every effort to contact all copyright holders. Any who for any reason have not been contacted are invited to write to the publishers so that a full acknowledgment may be made in subsequent editions of this work.

ISBN 1-873884-68-0

Designed by UFO Music Ltd

ufo music ltd.
email: ufomusic@dircon.co.uk

introduction

If The Beatles forever changed the way in which we listen to popular music, then, by the same token, *A Hard Day's Night* and *Help!* forever changed the way in which popular music was represented in the movies. Rock movies have always been unashamedly exploitative and budget-sensitive. From Sam Katzman's shoestring *Rock Around The Clock* through to those gaudy all-singing/all-dancing Elvis conveyor-belt dollar-magnets or, as in the case of *Easy Rider* - the pioneering use of a custom-compiled soundtrack to underscore the on screen drama, rock has proved an almighty box office come-on.

The Beatles movies were just as exploitative as any of these. In the case of *A Hard Day's Night* even more so. The *raison d'etre* behind shoving the Fab Four in front of a movie camera in the first instance, may have purely been an accounting exercise to turn a fast buck before the public rapidly lost interest(!), but, someone in the front office was astute enough to create a half-decent script and employ a director with genuine imagination.

Whereas, everyone from Bowie through to Dylan have allowed themselves to be shoe-horned into uncomfortable scenarios which ultimately did nobody any favours, The Beatles never once stepped out of character: all that was required of them was to perform a near-as-damn-it interpretation of their real selves or at least the persona the public recognised from television appearances and newsreel press conferences. Even when their image was psychedelicly animated for the purposes of *Yellow Submarine*, their fans were never once asked to suspend disbelief.

It seemed that almost immediately after *A Hard Day's Night* was screened Stateside, America's youth somehow managed to collectively grow its hair long overnight, squeeze into bizarre Carnabetian-styled clothes, form themselves into small groups and adopt cartoony brand names such as The Byrds, The Beau Brummels, The Young Rascals, The Lovin' Spoonful and The Monkees. The latter, shamelessly bought the whole enchilada. This wasn't a case of imitation as the sincerest form of flattery - this was Grand Larceny. In Britain, director John Boorman may have acknowledged Richard Lester's innovations when putting The Dave Clark Five through their paces in his 1965 production *Catch Us If You Can* (aka *Having A Wild Weekend*), but The Monkees' TV series, as devised by U.S. Pop Emperor Don Kirshner, hoovered up anything not nailed down and painted white only stopping short of having Mickey Dolenz, Davy Jones, Mike Nesmith and Peter Tork actually calling themselves John, Paul, George and Ringo.

If, tired and disillusioned, The Beatles came close to killing off their own myth with *Let It Be*, The Monkees virtually committed Hari Kari much earlier when begging to be taken seriously with their totally zonked *Head* (1968). Successful, though The Monkees' Beatle-clone TV series may well have been, it could never have existed without Richard Lester's two films to cannibalise. Same applied, in 1979, to obnoxious L.A.-based Fab-wannabes, The Knack ('My Sharona'), who never got further than a couple of excruciatingly-derivative pop videos and a universal slagging for their impertinence. Hollywood looked the other way. There will always be others.

Oasis may openly cite the Fab Four as an influence, but aside from their blistering on-stage encore of 'I Am The Walrus', they remain very much their own men. Whether or not they have their sights on a movie career is unknown. However, three decades on, Lester's influence still holds good, being rightly revered as the original architect for countless MTV-style pop videos.

In the final reckoning, no other act in history has so accurately book-ended their career in such a manner as The Beatles did with *A Hard Day's Night* and *Let It Be*. With these two films The Beatles defined the rock movie genre.

Leaving aside, the largely lacklustre concert-on-film approach, the only real alternative has been parody. However, so accurate were the black comedy spoofs of *The Rutles - All You Need Is Cash* and *This Is Spinal Tap* that they have virtually closed the book on this approach. If *A Hard Day's Night* captures the adrenaline-rush of Beatlemania as it happened, then the *Let It Be* docu-drama inadvertently became a sad epitaph, publicly bearing witness to their internal squabbling and lack of enthusiasm. However, few moments in the one hundred year history of film are as charmed as viewing *A Hard Day's Night* for the very first time. Even in today's somewhat jaded climate of been-there-seen-it-done-that-got-the T-shirt, it's youthful spirit of optimism remains unbowed. The fact remains, all things are still possible.

ROY CARR

1 THE SCAM

As with the best of scams, this one was virtually foolproof. Much to the annoyance of George Martin and Brian Epstein, it seems implausible that about the only people unable to foresee the potential in the Beatles were those running Capitol Records - the Los Angeles-based American arm of EMI. So, from February 1963 right up until the middle of 1964 - by which time the entire planet seemed to have succumbed to Beatlemania, Capitol's top brass were content for the first four Beatles singles and debut album to be released by Chicago R&B label Vee Jay, (Tollie, Oldies 45) and a small Philadelphia independent, Swan.

However, these labels more than served a purpose. It was almost like a covert operation, because even on their restricted marketing budgets, they effectively bonded The Beatles with America's young record buyers to a point where their fan base would soon reveal itself as second to none.

When, at the end of 1963, a sluggish Capitol belatedly got off its corporate backside and sprang into action, it was only because Brian Epstein had parleyed three high-profile slots on *The Ed Sullivan Show* for the lads. As for any long-term promotional field work, that had already been done for Capitol by these more enterprising smaller labels. All Capitol had to do was lazily dip their bread in what was soon to become gravy of untold richness.

In return for a meagre 10,000 bucks plus hotel and travel expenses, the Beatles would perform live for Sullivan on 9 and 16 February while a tele-recording would be inserted in the following week's transmission (23 February).

But all this, was still in the future. In the wake of the fan mayhem that accompanied the release of their fourth single - the signature sounding 'She Loves You', in August 1963, it was obvious that, even from a distance, The Beatles amounted to the biggest cash cow since the hip-shakin' pre-Army days of Elvis, six years earlier. Soon, everyone would be after a piece of the action.

BELOW Beatles' manager Brian Epstein, intended victim of US scandal sheet exposé.

How to mine the richest mother lode was the problem. One thing was certain, anyone capable of securing access to brand new Beatles recordings would have a license to print their own money in large denominations. There was just one obstacle. The Beatles still had two years to run on their Parlophone contract. No problem!

It was a clause in that contract excluding movie soundtracks that was soon to hit paydirt for George Ornstein - better known as user-friendly 'Bud'. The head of United Artists' movies in London, Bud Ornstein was both as razor sharp and minus-zero calculated as his position demanded. Obsessed by fame, social position and the desire to affect the mannerisms of the British aristocracy, Ornstein saw himself as a would-be Howard Hughes. For him it had been a question of marrying the boss's niece. His wife Gwen boasted Mary Pickford as her aunt, the very same legendary screen heroine who, years earlier, had founded United Artists' Studios in partnership with Douglas Fairbanks Sr and Charlie Chaplin.

To date, Ornstein's greatest achievement had been his decision to transplant the movie business from Hollywood to Europe - notably to cost-effective Spain where *The Pride and The Passion* starring Cary Grant, Frank Sinatra and Sophia Loren was the first of many productions to take advantage of such benefits as low overheads, good weather and cheap wine. In the process, Ornstein befriended Spain's fascist dictator General Franco along with other Continental café society celebrities such as exiled gangland mobster Lucky Luciano.

Despite his exotic taste in friends, Ornstein kept himself informed about everything relating to his business and was always prepared to listen to any scheme that could turn a fast buck. One such idea floated by UA Records' employee Noel Rodgers suggested that they both take a much closer look at these four lovable mop-tops who were giving young British girls severe attacks of the vapours.

At that time, it would have been difficult to ignore The Beatles. They weren't just another transient pop music diversion, but had become a genuine phenomenon embraced by the tabloid press to where they now rivalled the Royal Family - or anyone else for that matter - for daily front page column inches.

Ornstein prepared a few simple calculations to the comforting sound of cash registers ringing in his brain. Sign The Beatles to a three-picture deal and UA's record division legitimately picked up three soundtrack albums in the process; each containing at least half-a-dozen brand new Lennon and McCartney songs. As it transpired, they got eight!

Produced on a tight budget, such films would pay back their origination costs on UK rentals alone - the profit would be from the sale of the soundtrack albums. If, as Ornstein anticipated, the Fab Four ultimately broke stateside, then additional revenues would rapidly run into many millions. And that is precisely what happened.

Though UA wanted to make something a cut above such Sam Katzman-styled low budget exploitive rock 'n' roll quickies as *Rock Around The Clock* they were equally reluctant to stretch to the

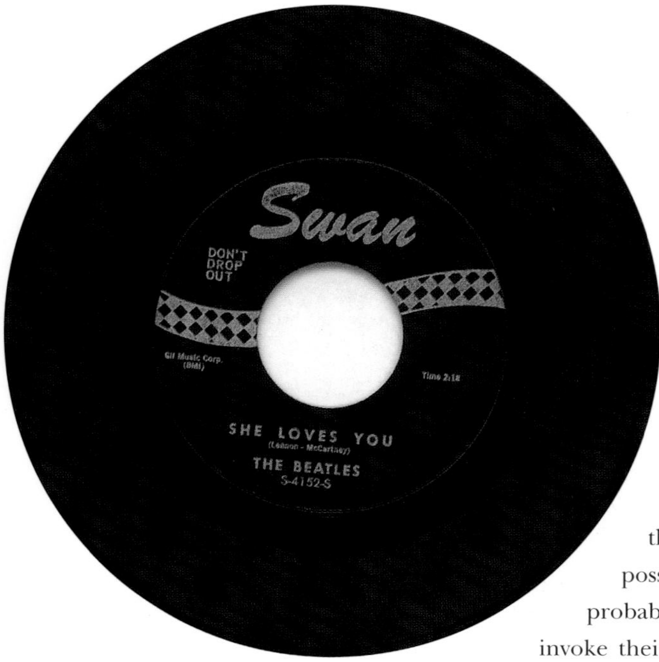

kind of higher production values lavished by 20th Century Fox on the Jayne Mansfield starrer, *The Girl Can't Help It* or a conveyor-belt Elvis drive-in popcorn epic.

Producing a Beatles movie was merely a means to an end - obtaining it's accompanying soundtrack album was the prime objective. Shoot it quickly in black and white for no more than £200,000 and a safe investment was almost guaranteed. Aside from the budget, there was one major proviso - the movie had to be finished and in the cinemas by the end of June 1964. The reason was that the American end of UA's operation felt there was a distinct possibility that by the following summer, The Beatles' appeal could quite probably have peaked. If that proved to be the scenario, UA could always invoke their get-out clause and scrap any future movies. **"So we had a terribly, terribly tight schedule,"** affirmed the soon-to-be-hired director Richard Lester.

On the strength of his success with a Peter Sellers vehicle, *The Mouse That Roared*, Ornstein commissioned independent producer Walter Shenson with the job of assembling the package. Next came the task of putting the offer to The Beatles' manager, Brian Epstein. Mindful of the budget at his disposal, Ornstein wanted to appear enthusiastic but not over-keen when meeting Epstein for the first time.

On a creative level, Epstein may well have projected the public image of a modern-day Svengali, but in reality, he was far from astute, business wise. Often, he was alarmingly incompetent, as in rapid succession he negotiated what proved to be a string of poor financial deals on behalf of his most prized clients. For instance, his original contract with Parlophone was risible, commencing at one penny per single with a 25 percent (one farthing) increment each year until it peaked at two pence. On album sales, the royalty amounted to a piffling four pence. Stateside, The Beatles received only six cents an album when anything from 25-50 cents would have been deemed reasonable. Nor did Epstein use either his initiative or power to renegotiate a more satisfactory rate when The Beatles' contract with EMI came up for renewal three years later.

However, at the time Epstein struck the original EMI deal he was a desperate man, fearful of losing both face and The Beatles as a result of being unable to secure for them the recording contract he had promised to deliver. The fact was, Epstein had been turned away by practically every label in town. In all probability, had he known how to, it's quite likely that Epstein would have gone as far as paying a label to sign his protégés. Indeed, unproven rumours suggested that Epstein offered to purchase enough copies of the Beatles' first release for his Liverpool store to more than cover EMI's expenditure.

In later years, these and numerous other business transactions ranging from the thorny subject of Beatles' merchandising through to tax shelter schemes may have cast a shadow of doubt over Epstein's honesty, but in actual fact, it was just a reflection of his continued inability to cut a half-decent deal.

ABOVE The Beatles' pre-Beatlemania release *'She Loves You'* on the US indie label, Swan.

ABOVE Having previously ignored the signs, Capitol Records finally got behind The Beatles with the single *'I Want To Hold Your Hand'*.

Neither Bud Ornstein or Walter Shenson were aware of this when they first approached Epstein in the summer of 1963. Anticipating a ruthless negotiator, they were prepared to offer up to 25 percent of net profits, only to be stopped dead in their tracks when, by way of an opening gambit, Epstein considered he was driving a hard bargain when he insisted he wouldn't budge for less that 7.5 percent! Ornstein was convinced that he had caught a real live one in Brian Epstein.

Fortunately, nothing was signed at this point. As things stood, it could have proved to be a one-sided arrangement were it not for Epstein's lawyer, David Jacobs, who revised the deal to what the producers originally had in mind. Unfortunately, Jacob's expertise was as a divorce lawyer, so the deal wasn't altogether to The Beatles' advantage. Had Epstein and Jacobs taken experienced legal counsel in such important matters, the deal would have been based on gross profits. Luckily for both Epstein and Jacobs, they weren't dealing with Hollywood sharks, so in time they received those monies to which they were justly entitled.

The next move was to create a suitable vehicle for The Beatles' screen debut. American-in-London, Richard Lester was assigned as the director and celebrated playwright Alun Owen drafted in to create an original screenplay. Before all this, The Beatles had vowed not to set foot on American soil, under any circumstances, until the public demanded their presence. And, that meant having a single firmly ensconced at Number One on the US charts. This they achieved with 'I Want To Hold Your Hand'. So when, on Friday, 7 February 1964, they stepped onto the tarmac of New York's Idlewild Airport they had fulfiled their biggest ambition to date. Even the gods couldn't have got the timing so precise.

Soon after the end of World War II, there had been a birth rate explosion which, by 1964, had resulted in seventeen-year-olds emerging as America's largest single age group. And, it was this vast number of grief-stricken teenagers, still in the painful throes

ABOVE Top US television host, Ed Sullivan, hasn't the faintest idea what his guests are talking about.

of recovering from John F. Kennedy's assassination the previous November, who recognised The Beatles as the perfect distraction. Even the Vietnam conflict was momentarily forgotten.

In such an atmosphere, The Beatles' sheer dynamism, their life energy and, above all, their unbridled optimism proved infinitely more intense than that first experienced in Britain. What's more they came as a user-friendly four-pack. Such was the magnitude of their media-grabbing impact that it was only comparable with a close encounter of the third kind. They were unique.

For all their charismatic appearance, strange-sounding voices and an ability to communicate on practically every level, The Beatles might as well have been extra-terrestrial visitors. In comparison, even the Second Coming would have only merited a couple of columns on page two.

Unbeknown to all but a few people, the whole Beatles escapade came close to disaster during their first expedition to the USA. There were always fears that Epstein's private life would one day become public. At times, those around Epstein were concerned that he seemed more preoccupied with sex than working in the best interests of his clients. Even before his association with The Beatles, Epstein was experienced in paying off plain clothed police officers who'd nabbed him cruising Liverpool's less reputable districts after dark. Sadly, this pattern would be repeated in London right up until his untimely death. Indeed, there was much speculation that Epstein's death was not suicide, but a bizarre S&M ritual abruptly terminated with disastrous results.

When The Beatles hit Manhattan, the gay fraternity saw to it that Brian Epstein's insatiable sexual appetite was constantly fulfiled as a stream of heavy traffic paraded through his suite, overlooking Central Park, at the Plaza Hotel. On the Saturday night before the taping of their third *Ed Sullivan* appearance, a photographer - employed by one of the more lurid 'screw-and-tell' magazines - abseiled down the exterior of the Plaza hopeful of catching the Fab Four cementing Anglo-American relationships with eager female fans. Instead, he discovered Epstein in the company of a legally under-age youth and his pants around his ankles. Click. Click. Click.

At the time, there were a lot of people on the periphery of The Beatles' organisation in whose interest it was to see that the group's wholesome image was steadfastly maintained. And, by any means necessary, there were those prepared to protect the success of the operation (including Capitol's $50,000 PR investment) in anticipation of the crock of gold at the end of the Beatle rainbow.

That's why over 2,000 screaming fans - many dressed in Beatles T-shirts given to them for free - suddenly appeared at Idlewild Airport, having been bussed in from the neighbouring boroughs to welcome the Fab Four to the New World when they first landed.

So, when business sources remote to the Fabs' immediate entourage were tipped off that a quick visit to a downtown Manhattan printer would be in their best interests, a crosstown car dash ensued that almost rivalled the best that *Bullit* had to offer. A word-in-the-ear had it, that, because of the Beatle connection, the unscrupulous publisher of a popular large-circulation scandal sheet was going to lead with a lurid front cover Epstein exposé. So confident was the magazine's smut-selling boss of an instant sell out, that he had farmed out the job to a printer with the capacity to meet the anticipated demand for several thousand extra copies. However, even before the story could be put on the presses, the printer became extremely ill at ease with the sexually explicit nature of the photographic evidence presented to him and felt in need of instant self-preservation therapy.

Having carefully viewed the incriminating evidence, the printer's two unhappy visitors adjusted their silk ties and swiftly moved into action. Discreet phone calls were made and individuals leaned on, resulting in the offending photographs and negatives immediately being procured and, happily, the need for large sacks of cement averted. Had the story been published, there is every reason to believe that, despite *The Ed Sullivan Show* generating the largest television viewing audience ever when 73,900,000 tuned in to see what all the fuss was about, The Beatles' mega-bucks bandwagon may have been permanently derailed Stateside and *A Hard Day's Night* scrapped less than a month before shooting commenced on 2 March.

2 The Film That Never Was: ONE
THE YELLOW TEDDYBEARS

Producer Sam Katzman set a precedent for cost cutting when, in 1956, he starred Bill Haley & His Comets in *'Rock Around The Clock'*, for what amounted to slightly more than spare change. And while it might have boasted one of the shortest shooting schedules imaginable, the fact that *'Rock Around The Clock'* raked in millions faster than they could be counted, won Katzman plaudits rather than scorn. With its effective use of technicolor, a first-rate cast and a genuinely witty script, 20th Century-Fox's widescreen entry, *'The Girl Can't Help It'* (1956), may have proved to be the best of the genre, but it didn't prompt a major studio rethink. Quite the reverse, Katzman promptly put calls through to Bill Haley and director Fred F. Sears and re-ran the same dollar-friendly formula as *'Don't Knock The Rock'*(1956).

Almost as if in homage to cheapskate ethics, Hollywood proceeded to crank out a succession of low-budget exploitive rock 'n' roll B-movies that made *'Rock Around The Clock'* look like an epic in comparison. Elvis may have had his moment on screen before going off to Europe to help defend mom and apple pie, but once back in cat clothes, he was shoe horned into mindless soufflés which, for the most part, boasted production values only marginally superior than those employed by television.

The Beatles, born of a generation brought up on this celluloid equivalent of junk food, suddenly found themselves not only pondering on which songs to schedule for their next single release, but discussing the prospects of a career in the movies. One thing was certain, they were determined not to put themselves into something that they would immediately regret.

OPPOSITE PAGE One-time night-club smoothie, Malcolm Mitchell opts for the Buddy Holly look and the gig of soundtracking *'The Yellow Teddybears'.*

Paul McCartney

'Very early on, we said to Brian Epstein that we wanted to be in films, but it had to be something decent. Something that we wouldn't be ashamed of later by which time it's too late! Quite early on there were a few things in the offing. Some were just rough ideas for a movie, while others were ready to go into production. One serious offer came from some London people who were making a film called *'The Yellow Teddybears'*. I think they wanted us to pop up in a couple of scenes to perform a song or two.'

'Naturally, we thought that it could be quite interesting, maybe even a bit of a laugh - just getting our four faces up there on the big screen. However, it wasn't as easy as that. In this instance, it turned out that either somebody else would write the music and we had to perform their songs or it might have been that part of the deal meant that we also had to give away the copyright to any new songs which were featured in the film. Whatever the reason, we immediately decided that was too much, so we turned that offer down and waited until something far better turned up.'

Produced and directed by Robert Hartford-Davis, *'The Yellow Teddybears'* was made in black and white and re-titled either *'Gutter Girls'* or *'The Thrill Seekers'* for export - which gives some indication as to the content. The synopsis centres on the fact, that amongst the knowing teenage girls at Peterbridge Grammar School, the wearing of a small yellow teddybear signifies the extent of their promiscuity. One pupil, Linda (Annette Whiteley) becomes pregnant and attends a party in London in order to earn enough money to pay for an abortion. She is accompanied by a naive classmate who returns to school after the weekend with a yellow teddybear pinned to her blouse.

A science teacher, Anne Mason (Jacqueline Ellis) eavesdrops on a conversation and learns of the common bond that units these badge-wearers. Linda's father prevents her from going ahead with her abortion while, at the same time, informing the school's headmistress of his daughter's dilemma. By way of a parting shot, he then disowns Linda who moves to London. In what proves to be a misplaced act of compassion, Anne Mason relates her own personal experiences to her pupils. She is censured by the school board and resigns. It doesn't get much better after that.

The music used in *'The Yellow Teddybears'* was written and performed by the former leader of the Malcolm Mitchell Trio; a successful variety act (much influenced by the Nat King Cole trio) which acted as a showcase for Mitchell's personality singing and jazz-tinged guitar style.

3 *The Young American* RICHARD LESTER

With the release of *'A Hard Day's Night'*, Richard Lester became the cinematic equivalent of the 'fifth' Beatle, in much the same manner that George Martin had acquired the 'honorary' title for the intelligent way in which he enabled the Fab Four to fully realise the musical aspects of their unique talents on record. Aside from The Beatles, the common bond shared by George Martin and Richard Lester was their professional association with Peter Sellers, Spike Milligan and other members of the The Goon show, the comedy radio show which ran in Britain from 1951-59. Martin was the producer of numerous comedy records, while Lester was the perpetrator of such television Goonery as *Idiot's Weekly, Price 2d, A Show Called Fred* and *Son Of Fred.* More importantly Lester was involved in Peter Sellers' privately made home movie *The Running, Jumping And Standing Still Film.*

Richard Lester was once described as looking as if his head was growing up through his hair, which is about as identikit accurate as one could get. A child prodigy at the age of two, Lester was said to be capable of not only reading but writing about 250 words. From there on, young Lester quickly developed an IQ of 186, entering university at 15, and graduating with a degree in clinical psychology amongst other academic credits. His father was Broadway playwright Elliott Lester while his mother was a respected soprano recitalist.

In rapid succession, young Lester formed a short-lived, five-part modern vocal group, became a CBS/TV floor manager, a morning disc jockey and, amongst other things, a puppet handler on Ed Sullivan's *Toast Of The Town.* Also capable of holding a tune on both piano and guitar, this ambitious Philadelphian arrived in the UK in 1955, before exploring Europe where, for a time, he eked out a living playing in Spanish and North African cafés.

Back in London, this 23-year old took over the production chores for Associated-Rediffusion Television's first jazz programme *Downbeat.* Later came *The Dick Lester Show* which also starred writer Alun Owen, but was doomed as a disastrous ad libbed attempt

ABOVE Beatles' movie director Richard Lester and the architect of today's MTV-style pop videos.

at TV Goonery. Short-lived it may well have been, but it attracted the attention of Peter Sellers who was on the look out in 1959 for someone capable enough to help transfer the Goons' surreal humour from radio to television.

Because the BBC owned the copyright in the title, *The Goon Show*, this other Fab Four of Sellers, Milligan, Harry Secombe and Michael Bentine came up with *Idiot's Weekly, Price 2d, A Show Called Fred* and *Son Of Fred*. More importantly, it resulted in the 11-minute *The Running, Jumping And Standing Still Film*. The latter was shot on two consecutive Sundays, using Peter Sellers' newly acquired 16mm movie camera. The location was a field in Muswell Hill, North London, hired for five pounds and the cast included Spike Milligan, Graham Stark, Mario Fabrizi and Bruce Lacey. Lester composed the accompanying music.

ABOVE Richard Lester and the Fabs share a private moment on the set of *'A Hard Day's Night'*.

Richard Lester

'When we put it together it was with absolutely no thought of commercial gain. The reason it was made was purely because Peter had bought a brand new 16mm movie camera and wanted to mess about with it. There was never an organised plan of doing anything with the edited film.'

That was until Sellers' friend - Daily Express TV critic Herbert Kretzmer - viewed it and immediately suggested they show it to a friend of his who selected films for the annual Edinburgh Festival. It was subsequently screened at this prestigious event, bought for the San Francisco Festival and then nominated for an Academy Award. Back in London, Roy Boulting picked it up for British Lion Films and it was shown in the News Theatre in Praed Street.

Richard Lester

'But, literally, when we made it, there were no plans to release it. Everyone loved it and said, if we ever want a 90-minute version we'll let you know, but they never did.'

BELOW Richard Lester begs Paul for the address of his tailor.

Many would later say *A Hard Day's Night* came close to this unmade version. To this day, it is seen as somewhat bizarre that an American was so clued into both the Englishness and eccentricity of the Goons' nonsensical surreal humour.

Richard Lester

'I think that there were three connections. One was that I had always, in comedy, found visual humour taking preference over verbal. Now, it sounds odd when you are talking about the people in question, because, my first connection would be with a radio show. But both Peter and Spike were visually orientated despite their verbal tricks. Spike especially. Throughout his career, Spike has shown himself to be extremely able of thinking visually, but at the beginning of our relationship he was adamant that comedy never works on television as a full-stop-don't-argue-we-me-mush!

'My God...my idol...right from my earliest school days was Buster Keaton whom I was blessed with working with on *Something Funny Happened To Me On The Way To The Forum* - his last film. Keaton was very much my hero as a director as much as anything else. I though that he was quite wonderful. When people used to say to me, but you're an American and don't get the references. I would reply, "no, I don't get the *specific* references"'

These references were things like Spike constantly inserting dubious cockney rhyming slang and Yiddish expressions into the script or name-checking 'Peter in Huge Hampton' during live TV transmissions. Vulgarities which not only went straight over Lester's head but also that of Associated-Rediffusion's middle-aged lady censor.

Richard Lester

'While I may have missed that, I shared the sense of the surreal with Spike. And that, to me, was universal. So whenever people said, "how can an American deal with English comedy?" I said, "it's the same - we're laughing at the same things. I may miss bits, but I have references of my historical background that he misses."'

ABOVE Paul and Richard discuss one of the scenes during the filming of *'Help!'*.

If, on occasion, the innumerable bawdy one-liners escaped him, subconsciously Lester had the ability to tap into the subtext.

Richard Lester
'It is easy to tune into a subtext if you are already tuned into the text, then probably it isn't that difficult to get the other bits fairly quickly. And, by and large, I honestly think that too much is written and spoken about the differences in comedy throughout the world.'

Lester has continued to work out of Twickenham Studios for most of his career which is but five minutes by car from his Thames-side house, ten minutes by boat and 25 minutes by foot.

Richard Lester
'It's a much more civilised way to behave than racing around Hollywood. I simply prefer England and I consider myself British. I'm not a patriot; I like the country too much to be described as that.'

Richard Lester and Joseph Losey split a series of 13 TV episodes of *Mark Sabre* between them during the 1956-57 season, but it was *It's Trad Dad* (1961) which afforded Lester his first opportunity to direct a major cinema feature. Rushed into production to cash-in on the Trad Jazz trend that had invaded the UK pop charts, *It's Trad Dad* proved to be an above-average let's-put-the-show-on-here teen exploitive shot in just four weeks

ABOVE On location in the middle of Salisbury Plain during *'Help!'*.

on a budget of only £65,000 (including Lester's salary of £1,500).

It's Trad Dad could have been assigned to the briefest of footnotes had it not been for Lester's innovative use of employing three cameras simultaneously to film two dozen musical items, featuring the likes of Helen Shapiro, Chubby Checker, Gene Vincent, Chris Barber and Acker Bilk. The well-told story is that the producer of *It's Trad Dad*, Milton Subotsky, initially mailed Lester 20 pages of notes. **"I read them and said, I think I can do something with this. I have a few ideas. As soon as you have the first draft of the script send it to me."** Lester was promptly informed that those 20 type written sheets represented the entire shooting script. The would-be director explained that there must be some mistake. He distinctly remembered being told that it was scheduled as a 90-minute movie with a page-a-minute shooting script. As things stood, there was a 70 page shortfall in the script. To his astonishment, Lester was instructed that he'd have to make do with what he had, so he better get on with it! **"That's all there was...and, that's how we left it."**

A three-camera shoot may have presented numerous technical difficulties, but Lester was working against a fast-ticking clock and a budget tighter than Chubby Checker's trousers. Re-takes were a luxury. But taking into account the kind of schedule he was given, it was the only feasible way of shooting that amount of footage in any given day. A triple camera shoot wasn't commonplace then and it is still rare today.

Richard Lester

'On every film I've made since *It's Trad Dad*, I've always used at least two cameras simultaneously. I have never understood why it was not the way that films were made. I see no disadvantages, only phenomenal advantages both artistically and emotionally in terms of the relationship between the film company and its actors. To keep them fresh, to keep them from becoming bored with the actual process of shooting any movie which can often be very slow.'

It is a technique, Lester insists, that worked to even greater effect during the making of yet another tightly budgeted/short schedule production - *A Hard Day's Night*.

4 *The Indian Rubber Man*
ALUN OWEN

Alun Owen was once described as **'a man who swears like a trooper but writes like an angel.'** Three years before he was approached to write the screenplay for *A Hard Day's Night*, Owen's self-image was as a **'Bohemian with working class roots.'** Born in Liverpool on 24 November, 1925, of Welsh parents, Alun Davies Owen spent the first eight years of his life in North Wales, after which, the family moved backed to Liverpool.

Following a two-year stint, during World War II, as a 'Bevin Boy', (Ernest Bevin recruited thousands of men to work down the mines as part of the war effort), in the coal mines of South Wales, Owen drifted into the theatre when he joined the Perth repertory company as a £4-a-week assistant stage manager. It was here that Owen met and quickly married a girl named Mary. They were both just 16 at the time.

In between jobs as a waiter, lorry driver's mate and ship's steward, the next dozen years saw Owen undertaking blink-and-you've-missed-him acting roles on television (prototype soap opera *The Grove Family*) and in movies (*I'm All Right Jack*). Tours of Ireland with 'fit-up' theatrical companies that included Kenneth Haigh and Harold Pinter sharpened his edge when he branched out as a comedian in *The Idiot's Weekly* and *Son Of Fred*. Later on, he became a stooge for the comedian Arthur Askey. Early in his career, Alun Owen had been highly critical of Wales. In 1960, he insisted:

> 'Liverpool and Wales... they're the two things I really know, and yet I'm not completely at home in either. Though Welsh was my first language - I couldn't speak English at all till I went to school at five - I now write in English, and even dream in English.'

> 'I love Wales, and I used to have a great romantic thing about Welsh, but at the same time I hate so much about the Welsh: the over-adjectivalisation of the Welsh, who never use one word when three or four

will do, so that all truth and feeling gets lost under a torrent of words; the fake Welsh nationalists who don't actually speak Welsh ("Well, of course, it was our first language, but somehow we stopped speaking it, you know"); the awful indeed-to-goodness stereotype which the Welsh have imposed on the rest of the world, and now they've got stuck with it.'

BELOW Alun Owen, *'A Hard Day's Night'* screenwriter and a man of letters.

Owen's first full-length play, *Progress In The Park*, began life as a BBC radio production. It reached the stage when, in 1959, Joan Littlewood presented it first at the Theatre Royal, Stratford and later at the Royal Court in Chelsea. In 1961, Owen's play arrived in the London's West End at the Saville Theatre in Shaftesbury Avenue. *Progress In The Park* was Owen's run at the Romeo and Juliet theme: the starcrossed love of a young Protestant boy for a Roman Catholic girl.

The budding playwright's next effort, *The Rough and Ready Lot*, was an ensemble piece revolving around a group of mid-19th Century British mercenaries sheltering in a South American monastery where they argued over the ethics of the bloody killing of the South American Indians by the Conquistadors. As *No Trams On Lime Street, After The Funeral, Lena, O My Lena, The Ruffians* and *The Strain* (the latter concerned with gang warfare in Liverpool) affirmed, it was to be as much his work for television - as any other medium - that earned Owen a reputation as one of the most perceptive writers of the day. Incidentally *No Trams On Lime Street* and *Lena, O My Lena* also launched the career of actress Billie Whitelaw.

At the time Alun Owen was commissioned to create *A Hard Day's Night*, he was also working on the book for Lionel Bart's upcoming Liverpudlian musical, *Maggie May* as well as drafting a new play. His appointment was made official on 30 October, 1963, while The Beatles were on tour in Sweden. The Beatles' press officer, Tony Barrow informed the media:

'Having got Alun Owen to write it is the best possible move for us. He is probably the best writer in Britain today writing about the Liverpool scene. He has had two first-class plays on TV about Liverpool and youngsters. We have turned down numerous offers from film companies waiting until just the right thing came along.'

Walter Shenson, the producer for The Beatles' yet-to-be-titled movie debut added:

'We see them as black-and-white people. Alun Owen is going to spend a lot of time with the boys and create characters for them that reflect their own. We want to put over their non-conformist, slightly anarchist characters. We want to present their almost Goon-like quality. We are taking a lot of care about this because we don't want any junk, any sort of cheap quickie. I look upon this film as having world wide popularity. The beat these kids dig is international.'

RIGHT The Beatles experiment with a new image make-over.

OPPOSITE PAGE George, Alun and John - doesn't quite have the same ring to it.

Later, Alun Owen offered his own comments on how he intended to craft the storyline.

> 'We're not going to have a story that ends up at the (London) Palladium with the vicar smiling and giving the thumbs-up sign from the stalls. Nothing like that. The thing about the boys is this great joy of being ALIVE that they put across. They're so ebullient - it knocks me out. They affirm. They aren't a sleazy image of pimply adolescence...these fellows really LIVE. They swing. They're with it. I'll be travelling with them, studying them, watching their effect on the people they meet. This film will be moulded round them, round their personalities. In the film I want them to be searching for something. Not success, but looking for something or somebody. At least I come from Liverpool, grew up there and know the people. You know, the thing about Liverpool people - and that includes the boys - is that we're resilient. Throw us on the floor and we'll bounce right back. We're the India-rubber men of Great Britain!'

And so Alun Owen put pen to paper.

5

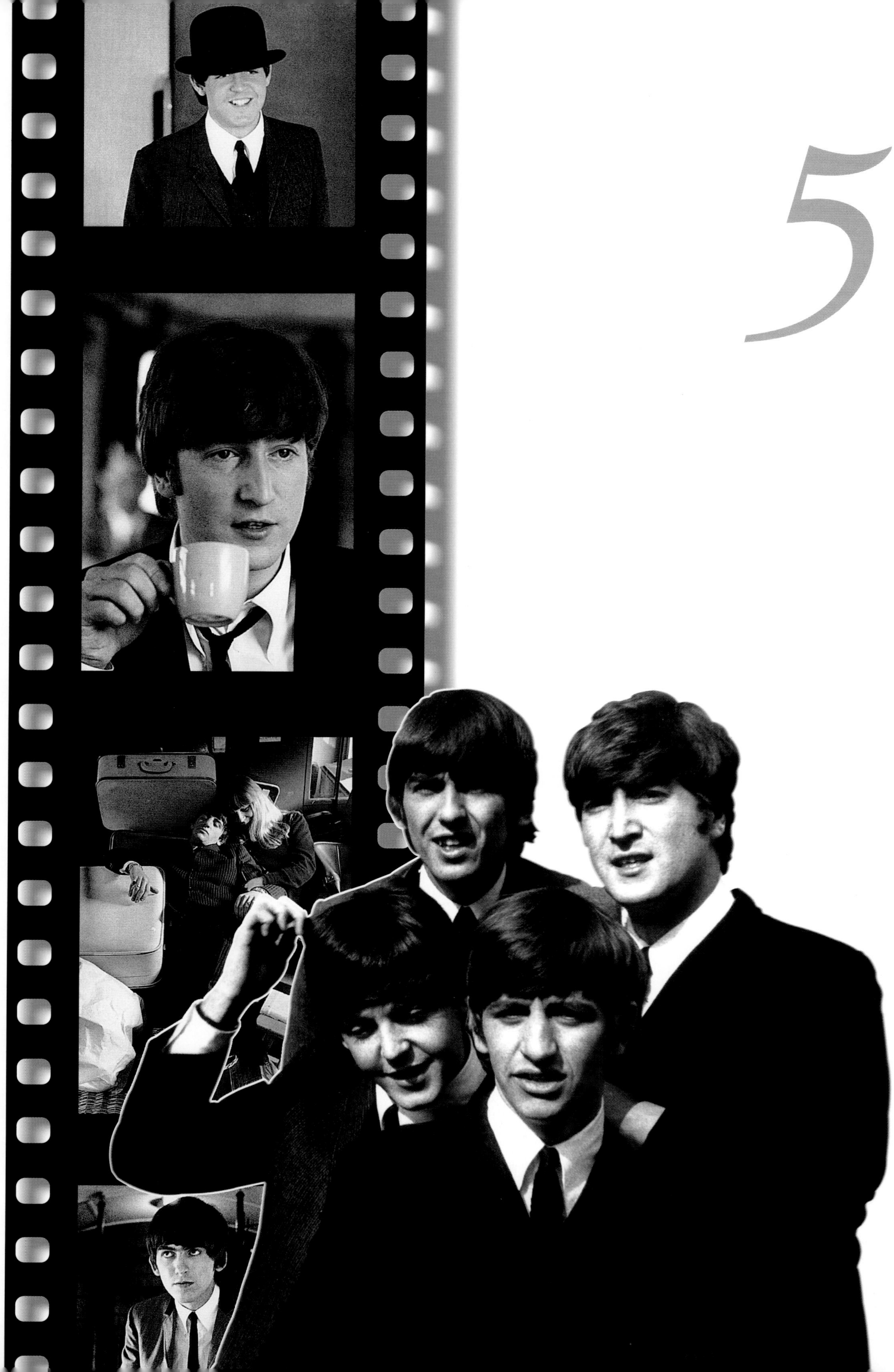

A HARD DAY'S NIGHT

'Doesn't matter if you're in a group or not, at one time or another, everyone has imagined themselves starring in either a rock film or a James Bond movie. We weren't any different, except suddenly we got the opportunity to do just that...make a movie! But what did we know about making movies? Absolutely nothing except that we all instinctively knew if something was crap. And there were a lot of crap rock movies about - *Teenage Millionaire* for one.'
John Lennon

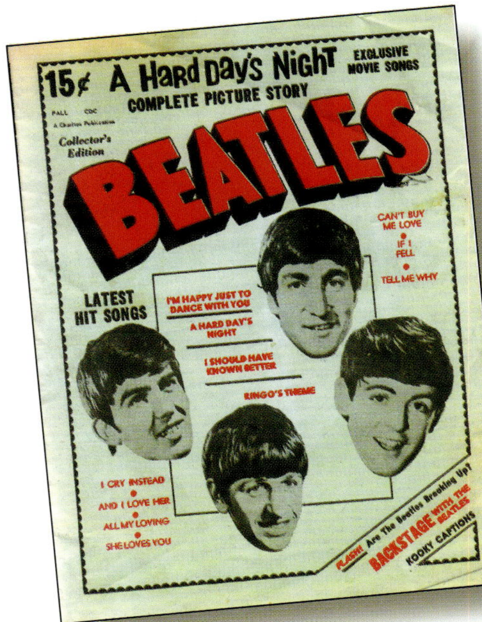

A Hard Day's Night was to become the first-ever movie in history to go into profit while it was still before the cameras. The events that led up to this began in October 1963 when Richard Lester first met The Beatles. However, it wasn't until January 1964 that their relationship was placed on a professional level. The Beatles, as it transpired, were familiar with both *The Running Jumping And Standing Still Film* and *It's Trad Dad* - the latter mainly because it contained footage of seminal rocker Gene Vincent whom they had befriended in their Cavern-era days. For, *It's Trad Dad*, Vincent swopped his familiar black 'biker' outfit to appear clad in white leathers performing *Spaceship To Mars*.

LEFT Patti Boyd (Georges future wife) catches Georges eye as The Beatles rehearse a song for *'A Hard Day's Night'*.

John Lennon

'We'd made it clear to Brian that we weren't interested in being stuck in one of those typical nobody-understands-our-music plots where the local dignitaries are trying to ban something as terrible as the Saturday Night Hop. The kind of thing where we'd just pop up a couple of times between the action...all smiles and clean shirt collars to sing our latest record and once again at the end when the local mayor has been convinced that we're not all mass-murderers or, worse still, about to start shagging some young Sunday School teacher in the Town Hall flower beds...We all know that scene so well...where he and a bunch of senile town councillors and the Police Chief start dancing around all over the place like those bloody *Thunderbirds* puppets...Never mind all your pals, how could we have faced each other if we had allowed ourselves to be involved in that kind of movie?'

Paul McCartney

'We'd only released a few singles and a couple of albums but we'd now reached the position where The Beatles were big enough for producers to approach us and ask if we'd like to make a full-length movie on our own terms. Not bad going for a bunch of scruffs who'd only recently come down south to London from Liverpool? We discussed this with Brian on a number of occasions and he asked if we had any ideas of our own. The only person we could think of was, whoever made that *Running Jumping And Standing Still Film*? Who did that, 'cause it was brilliant ?'

'The thing was, we all really loved that Goons film so, right away, that was an indication of the kind of direction we were all interested in. It might look a bit dated now, but it was fabulous back then. Basically, it was just what we liked. We could relate to the humour wholeheartedly. Brian discovered that it had been made by Richard Lester and so we said, well he's all right by us...we're really up for this one!'

Once Walter Shenson's deal with Epstein and the Beatles had been pacted, he approached Lester and asked, **"who can we get to write to screenplay?"** *Til Death Do Us Part* creator, Johnny Speight had been Lester's original choice to script The Beatles' movie debut. However, prior commitments prevented Speight from accepting the commission. As to which direction Londoner Speight might have steered them is open to all manner of speculation.

ABOVE Ringo and John relax with friend and photographer Astrid Kirchherr in between takes.

Richard Lester

'My second choice was Alun Owen who had been my partner on *The Dick Lester Show* and who, by that time, had written *No Trams In Lime Street* for television. When I first approached Johnny Speight, I explained that my brief was to make a 'factional' movie. And, even though what I had in mind was a loosely fictionalised documentary, in order to do these jumps into surrealism that is necessary to make songs interesting, I needed to insert a little burst of the surreal into the film that were not in the script.'

'But it was always clear that if you're going to play games with time and space for music, you need to warn the audience of its coming. A perfect example is the performance, on the train, in the baggage cage when The Beatles suddenly switch from playing cards to singing *I Should Have Known Better.* Three or four minutes before that sequence, there's this scene where, first, The Beatles are in the carriage and then suddenly there's this quick shot of them outside the carriage, running and cycling and, banging on the window to be let in. It's just a little thing to let the audience know that all is not just documentary.'

ABOVE There always seems to be more hanging around than actual filming.

ABOVE RIGHT John and George sign yet more autographs as they leave the George V Hotel, Paris.

Once Alun Owen had accepted the gig, he went along with Lester and Shenson to meet the Beatles at the Playhouse Theatre where they were recording their radio show for the BBC.

Richard Lester
'They knew that I was a jazz enthusiast - a really pathetic jazz player, and, I think that in some way it helped. Also they knew all about *It's Trad, Dad.* Anyway, there were enough connections that it seemed to be alright from the outset.'

Lester, Shenson and Owen then travelled to Paris in January 1964 to discuss the project with the would-be movie stars. The occasion was the start of an 18-day season The Beatles were playing at L'Olympia Théâtre (15 January - 4 February) with top French pop star Sylvie Varten and US hitmaker of *If I Had A Hammer*, Trini Lopez.

Richard Lester
'We stayed on the same floor as them in the George V Hotel, went backstage as they did their soundcheck and the film was writing itself right there in front of our eyes. We just took the dirty bits and cut them out!'

According to Lester, when they first met there was scarcely any communication at all: **"We sat and looked at each other for two days. Then I had a lot to drink and started to play the piano. We started laughing."** Of the three members of the visiting party, Shenson appeared to be the easiest for The Beatles to satirise and send up so that Lester and Owen had a much easier ride. **"Walter enjoyed it. It was a way of them testing us while at the same time bonding themselves."**

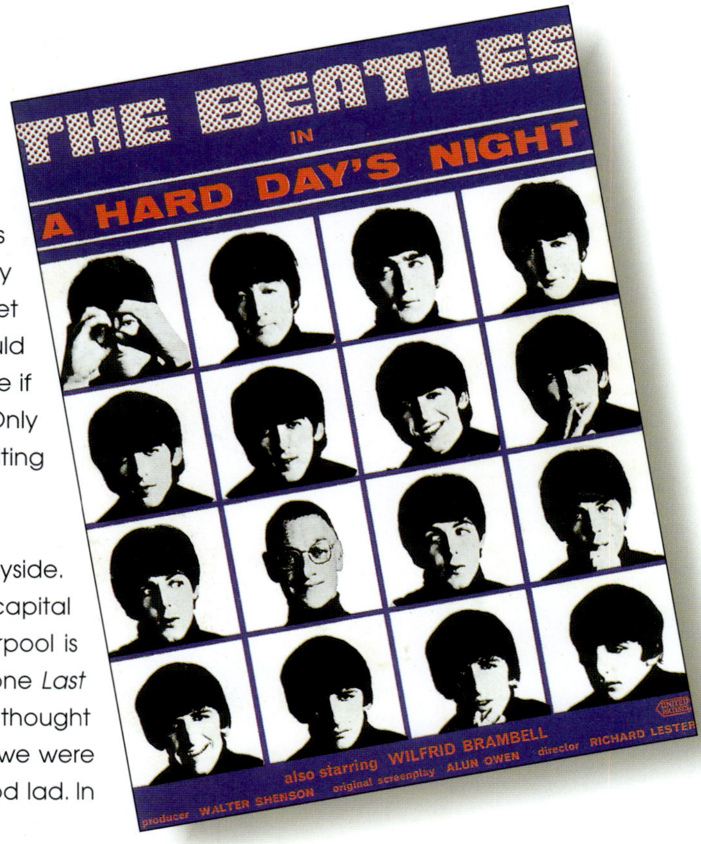

Paul McCartney

'Initially, when the question of a script arose, one or two names were put forward. As Johnny Speight was unavailable, they suggested Alun Owen and we said to Brian, why don't we get Alun to hang out with us for a few days. Not only so that we could check him out to see if we liked him but, just as important, to see if he could pick up a little of our swing...understand our ways. Only then would we really know if Alun was the right person to be writing the script.'

'For starters, it was a plus that Owen had been raised on Merseyside. Liverpool being the capital of Wales...for some, but then it's the capital of most places including Ireland!!! For many Welsh people, Liverpool is their London - the Metropolis. The thing is, Owen had recently done *Last Train From Lime Street* with Billie Whitelaw for television and we thought that wasn't bad. So, he already had a bit of credibility as far as we were concerned, then, when we met him we liked him...he was a good lad. In fact, he remained a lovely man right up until he died.'

'Anyway, he hung out with us...started chatting to us and we started having a laugh and it was a laugh...that was the big secret, he wasn't too above us and pretty soon we felt that he was starting to get the idea of what we were about. The important thing is that Owen didn't attempt to turn us into characters that we weren't. Those parts of the film where they did, just didn't work and they ended up on the cutting room floor. The secret to the success of *A Hard Day's Night* was that there was a little of our own personalities in it.'

Just how comfortable did The Beatle actors feel with Alun Owen putting words into their mouths?

Paul McCartney

'We all quite liked it, there were only one or two moments when we didn't...like 'grotty' wasn't a word that we actually said. It was one of Alun Owen's made-up things...Alun doing a sort of Liverpool, Irish, Welsh, Celtic slang. 'Grotty' was just not a word we would have used. But it was very good...other than that, we were comfortable...Alun's script was quirky and it reflected something of how we liked to think we were.'

Coupled with Richard Lester's innovative camera work, *A Hard Day's Night* forever freeze-framed an image of The Beatles the world still clings to affectionately.

ABOVE The British programme for the film *'A Hard Day's Night'.*

Paul McCartney

'To a certain extent that's true, but it was a film, so despite what some people thought, it wasn't real life...we understood that. It wasn't like we were thick. John being an art student, me doing a bit of sixth form literature and studying plays and poetry. We were very aware of films. We all had favourites and they tended to be French movies or rather good British and American movies, so when it came down to it, I think we had pretty good taste. *A Hard Day's Night* fitted quite well into that. If anything, we didn't think it was quite far out enough...we tried to get Dick to do a couple of things that didn't quite come off. I remember one of the things we wanted him to do was where...like in some of those spaghetti western and kung fu movies, we would intentionally badly post-sync some stuff and alter all the words to add just a bit more surrealism to the whole thing. But due to both the tight budget and the shooting schedule, we just didn't have the time for all that.'

A Hard Day's Night was scheduled to begin production on 2 March and had to be finished in time for its Royal Premiere on 6 July.

Richard Lester

'This meant we only had seven weeks shooting and then had to cut it and dub it and get a final print ready for the end of June. It was all a blur...nobody really had time to stop and think over what they were doing. But the incredible speed with which it was made worked to its benefit - if it's gonna work, it's gonna work right from the beginning and this happened with *A Hard Day's Night*.'

BELOW George going like the clappers.

Paul McCartney
'It didn't feel at all fast to us simply because we didn't know how long it took to make a movie. They kept saying, "it's only eight weeks"...fine, yeah...but that was a long time in our life. Eight weeks was equivalent to a year - we could have done a couple of tours, written a few new songs and cut an album...maybe, even do a few others things! But, to the people working on the film set, eight weeks was a comparatively short time. We didn't know any better, we just thought, wow - this is taking a long time!'

Whereas, in the UK, Beatlemania had steadily built up over a period of 18 months, Stateside - after initially being ignored - The Beatles' acceptance was of the overnight variety and the shock waves even more severe than when Elvis had first exploded into the nation's living-rooms back in 1956. Following their initial conquest of North America, the Beatles arrived back in Britain on Saturday, 22 February 1964. Without pausing for a second breath, they spent the whole of the following day tele-recording half a dozen songs and three comedy sketches with popular comedy duo Mike and Bernie Winters for transmission on *Big Night Out* (ABC-TV) the following week on 29 February.

After a day off, and with just one week to go before shooting commenced on the set of their first feature film, The Beatles reconvened at Abbey Road on Tuesday, 25 February (George's 21st birthday) for three consecutive days of intensive recording. The task at hand was to sort out potential material for the upcoming soundtrack to their screen debut. Also pencilled in was an additional three-hour session (1 March) the night before they were due to assemble on Paddington railway station in their new role as movie stars. Others might have cracked under such constant pressure.

BELOW The Beatles chance their luck with a British Rail breakfast.

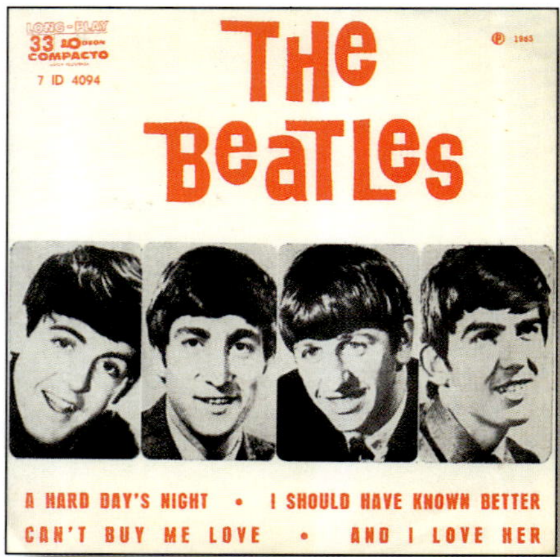

Paul McCartney
'We were kinda used to that by then - that was the way we worked. An eight weeks' filming schedule seemed like a very long time to us - everyone on the set seemed to hang around for ever. Now, the one thing The Beatles didn't do was hang about.'

'When John and I were told to write something, we got on with it. Normally, Brian Epstein would just ring us up and say, "you're all in the studio the week after next, so you better write something next week." So, that's exactly what we'd do. We'd just take a week off and some days I'd go to John's home and others he would come over to mine and every day we met we'd write at least one new song so, by the end of the week, we'd have these seven songs and in the meantime, we'd each be knocking off a few songs independently. John would be knocking off *I Should Have Known Better* on his own and I'd also be doing the same. We finished it all pretty quickly and soon had more than enough songs. It wasn't like we were writing a soundtrack, we were just writing Beatles songs that just happened to be a soundtrack to a movie.'

Surprisingly, this songwriting team hadn't methodically stockpiled a cache of partly completed songs; an assortment of middle-eights, bridges, and catchy hooks to call upon whenever they found themselves up against the tightest of deadlines.

Paul McCartney
'Most of the songs that John and I wrote together were kinda pulled out of the air. That was one of the things about John and me that I still marvel at...because we had been 16-year-olds together; he'd come over to my house and we'd smoke Ty-Phoo tea in my dad's pipe and, because we'd done all that, by the time we got around to *A Hard Day's Night*, we sort of expected that when we sat down together to write a song we'd have a bit of fun, simply because we were used to it. That was how we did what we did. Any ideas that we had lurking wouldn't be so much middle-eights, but rather a title, or perhaps an opening line. We'd just kick it off and within three or four hours we'd both feel very disappointed if we didn't have a finished song that we both knew and could sing the next day. There weren't any cassette recorders so we just had to remember them. And, we always did. The only place to bank it was in your head - a safety deposit box in there. Next day you woke up and thought, that was a good 'un - sang it again a couple of times so that you kinda knew it. They nearly all came very quickly, there were only one or two later on that were a slight struggle, but mostly they never took more than one day when ever John and I sat down together. Fact was, we'd become rather good at it by then!'

ABOVE The Brazilian version of the single *'A Hard Day's Night'*.

OPPOSITE PAGE Patti Boyd and the lads cop a drag between scenes.

The songs having been written for the soundtrack, just four days were set aside to record such all-important material.

25 FEBRUARY

First, time was spent overdubbing Paul's lead vocal and George's guitar part to 'Can't Buy Me Love' which had originally been recorded in Paris, on Wednesday, 29 January 1964. Next up was 'You Can't Do That' (John) and their new single (their sixth) was in the can. Their attention now turned to first attempts at 'And I Love Her' (Paul) and 'I Should Have Known Better' (John).

26 FEBRUARY

The Beatles recut 'And I Love Her' and 'I Should Have Known Better'. A third attempt on the latter was included in the following day's schedule.

27 FEBRUARY

The day's work started with a satisfactory re-make of 'I Should Have Known Better' followed by 'Tell Me Why' and 'If I Fell'.

28 FEBRUARY

The Beatles placed their soundtrack sessions on hold for the day, switching studios from Abbey Road to the BBC radio's Piccadilly Studio in London's West End to tape eight songs for their show *From Us To You*, which was scheduled for transmission on Easter Monday, 30 March.

29 FEBRUARY

A Saturday and a leap year, and, with filming due to begin on Monday, The Beatles saw the shooting script for the first time.

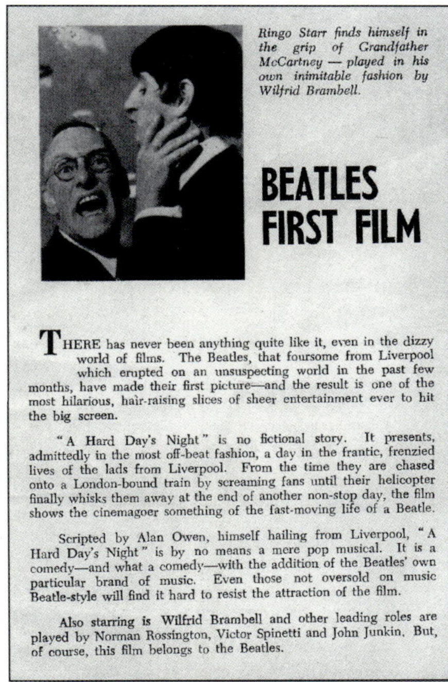

Ringo Starr finds himself in the grip of Grandfather McCartney — played in his own inimitable fashion by Wilfrid Brambell.

BEATLES FIRST FILM

THERE has never been anything quite like it, even in the dizzy world of films. The Beatles, that foursome from Liverpool which erupted on an unsuspecting world in the past few months, have made their first picture—and the result is one of the most hilarious, hair-raising slices of sheer entertainment ever to hit the big screen.

"A Hard Day's Night" is no fictional story. It presents, admittedly in the most off-beat fashion, a day in the frantic, frenzied lives of the lads from Liverpool. From the time they are chased onto a London-bound train by screaming fans until their helicopter finally whisks them away at the end of another non-stop day, the film shows the cinemagoer something of the fast-moving life of a Beatle.

Scripted by Alan Owen, himself hailing from Liverpool, "A Hard Day's Night" is by no means a mere pop musical. It is a comedy—and what a comedy—with the addition of the Beatles' own particular brand of music. Even those not oversold on music Beatle-style will find it hard to resist the attraction of the film.

Also starring is Wilfrid Brambell and other leading roles are played by Norman Rossington, Victor Spinetti and John Junkin. But, of course, this film belongs to the Beatles.

1 MARCH
Just three hours was all it took for The Beatles to record 'I'm Happy Just To Dance With You' (Paul) followed by a pulverising one take of 'Long Tall Sally' (Paul) which served notice on the Little Richard original, before finally working up their own version of a song which had already proved a hit for Billy J Kramer and The Dakotas - 'I Call Your Name' (John).

The following morning, the first scenes were shot at Paddington station. Later, during the week, Richard Lester was handed copies of the tapes, nine songs in all, from which he chose, 'Can't Buy Me Love', 'I Should Have Known Better', 'If I Fell', 'I'm Happy Just To Dance With You', 'And I Love Her', 'Tell Me Why' and 'You Can't Do That'. As things turned out, 'I Call Your Name' and 'Long Tall Sally' were dropped while later on 'You Can't Do That' had to be scrapped from the final cut.

Richard Lester
'That was an attempt which we thought of really too late to adequately prepare for - and that was to film 'You Can't Do That' as a stop-motion dance sequence featuring the Lionel Blair Dancers on stage with The Beatles. In those days, to do proper stop-motion, we needed a particular claw-pull camera that was much more precise than our camera. We tried to fake it using all the wrong equipment and weren't able to do it and it fell apart with the result that we wasted half-a-day of quite a short shooting schedule.'

ABOVE LEFT Patti Boyd appears totally absorbed by Paul's comments.

ABOVE Wilfred Brambell and Paul, seen here with the addition of some false facial hair, take a few hints from director Richard Lester.

ABOVE RIGHT John Lennon sees for himself that Paul's screen Grandfather (Wilfred Brambell) is very clean.

The recording of the title tune, 'A Hard Day's Night' (John) didn't occur until Tuesday, 16 April 1964 when, as legend has it, Ringo Starr came up with what was to become the film's title, as a result of a casual witticism. With George's shock-of-surprise opening guitar chord of Gm7 add 11, Ringo's choppy drummimg, a strident instrumental break that features unison guitar and piano plus a perfectly focused vocal track, movie themes don't come much better than this. Up until that moment, just about everyone had been trying to come up with an instantly catchy title. Most of them were forced and unsuitable. Among the alternative suggestions had been 'Beatlemania', 'The Beatles Film', 'It's A Daft, Daft, Daft, Daft World' (George), 'Oh, What A Lovely Wart!' (Paul).

Then, one evening after a particularly heavy day on the film set, one of the four began to mutter, **"We've had a hard...",** at which point Ringo uttered those immortal words: **"A hard day? Look at that clock. You mean a hard day's night, don't you?"**

The first two days in June were devoted to recording the remaining non-soundtrack material for the British version of *A Hard Day's Night* and the only album of all Lennon-McCartney material the Beatles ever released.

1 JUNE

With legendary first generation American rock 'n' roller, Carl Perkins observing from the Abbey Road control room, The Beatles quickly moved from covering Perkins' Sun label hit 'Matchbox' (Ringo), to 'I'll Cry Instead' (John/Paul) - a Lennon song that was dropped from *A Hard Day's Night* but nevertheless still found its way on to the US version of the soundtrack. This was probably due to the fact that, at one point, 'I'll Cry Instead' was going to accompany the action, when The Beatles burst out of the theatre, scramble down an iron staircase and are filmed (often in rapid motion) running and cavorting wildly all over a field. For the final cut, 'I'll Cry Instead' was dropped in favour of 'Can't Buy Me Love' Next up was a cover of Larry Williams' 'Slow Down' (John). The day's work finished with 'I'll Be Back' (John).

2 JUNE

Recorded this day were 'Any Time At All' (John), 'When I Get Home' (John) and 'Things We Said Today' (Paul).

Ever since the very early days of the Keystone Cops the comedy chase has been the cinema's most enduring device. And, *A Hard Day's Night* didn't buck the system. During a Scandinavian tour, John Lennon likened The Beatles lot as just rapidly exchanging one interior for another...**"it was a room and a car and a car and a room and a room and a car"**.

So crucial to the plot was Lennon's statement that Alun Owen incorporated it into the actual script when McCartney's screen Grandfather bemoans: **"I thought I was going to get a change of scenery and so far I've been in a train and a room and a car and a room and a room and a room."**And it was the exhausting pace of this gold fish-bowl existence that Lester was determined to capture in his exaggerated day-in-the-life escapade. Lester had seen for himself that at no time were they allowed to enjoy what was supposed to be success. The truth was The Beatles had now become prisoners of their own good fortune. By their own admission, it wasn't uncommon for all four of them suddenly to retreat to the hotel bathroom for nothing more ominous than to escape the mayhem taking place all around them for just a moment.

Realising that this went on practically every day of their life, Lester wanted to compress this feeling of claustrophobia into the plot of *A Hard Day's Night*. This was the price they paid and the only time they were truly happy was when making music.

In much the same way as, during the introduction to the cult television series, *The Prisoner*, Patrick McGoohan would run along a deserted beach and shout, 'I am not a number, I am a free man!', likewise, the scene where the Beatles run themselves ragged in the field while 'Can't Buy Me Love' blares out from the soundtrack was symbolic of them asserting their personal freedom...creating their own space. This was to be the core of *A Hard Day's Night* while the semi-fictional manifestation of the Fab Four is the way the world would forever perceive The Beatles.

The running jokes were clear cut and strategically placed throughout the script: knowing references about Paul's cantankerous Grandfather (Wilfred Brambell), and how ''e's very clean' as though there's something about that statement that nobody wished to discuss in detail.

Similarly, Norm (Norman Rossington) and Shake (John Junkin) as knockoutabout versions of The Beatles' real-life roadies (Neil Aspinall and Mal Evans) arguing about the former's physical shortcomings: fall-guy Shake explaining to his Bolshie vertically-challenged cohort, "I'm not taller - you're shorter!"

ABOVE A Mexican billboard poster for the film.

Finally, the opening gambit of Victor Spinetti's inspired portrayal of a paranoid television producer: "If you think I'm unsuitable then let's have it out in the open. I can't stand these backstage politics." Or, when instructing a go'fer to bring him a bottle of milk and tranquillisers: "I see it all now, it's a plot,"

While integral to the plot, such vignettes were still somewhat of a minor distraction, it was the presence of The Beatles that illuminated a scene and, as Walter Shenson said, you couldn't take your eyes off them.

The techniques that Lester applied were far more sophisticated than the actual content, which was purposely slap-dash and made to look as breathlessly spontaneous as possible. And, in some instances, it replicated the hit-the-ground-running *vérité* quality of the US press conferences and general madness that filmmakers Albert and David Maysles had captured in their TV reportage of The Beatles' first US visit in *Yeah! Yeah! Yeah! The Beatles In New York* (aka *What's Happening! The Beatles In The USA*).

As in any good cinematic chase, the pace never slackened, only momentarily easing up for tramp-like Ringo's 'silent' riverside cameo (during which, Ringo later confessed, he was pissed out of his brains having arrived on set straight from a night on the town). It was this as much as anything that prompted the movie world to extol Ringo as a 'natural actor'. He may well have been just that, but he was never afforded a suitable script to test him truly, instead he was shoe-horned into dumb star-studded vehicles such as *Candy* and *Magic Christian* and later, even worse.

The sight of The Beatles on film inspired countless American garage bands

ABOVE The guitar song book featuring all the songs from the film.

ABOVE RIGHT It's Ringo's turn to check out if Wilfred Brambell is as 'clean' as everyone insists.

such as the fledgling Byrds to reinvent themselves. As David Crosby readily admits,

> '*A Hard Day's Night* was a turning point in my life. We all went to see it together...(Roger) McGuinn and I and Gene (Clark) and Chris Hillman, and maybe Michael Clark too! I came out and swung around a post arm's length going 'Yes!' I went into that movie and came out knowing what I wanted to do with the rest of my life.'

Years later, seeing *A Hard Day's Night* had a similar effect on New York punk rockers, The Ramones.

Richard Lester's innovative camera work on *A Hard Day's Night* quickly proved to be a meal-ticket for those who trailed in his dust. Top of the heap were the makers of *The Monkees* TV series who unashamedly plundered Lester's oeuvre without ever matching his quick-witted sense of visual humour or his ability to pace the action effectively which he positioned bang in the centre of each frame. Three decades on, and Richard Lester's techniques continue to be applied to innumerable MTV-style pop videos.

ABOVE The original US billboard poster for the film.

> **Richard Lester**
> 'I am more visual than verbal and I am inclined to film scenes in an architectural way - almost absolutely front on...very much like an architect's plan. Sometimes very acute angles, but never anything in between - despite all the talk of "tricksy camera".That's all nonsense, I never move the camera. Neither did Buster Keaton or Jacques Tati. What you do is make the space around the actors either funny or dramatic. If you're moving the camera at the same time, you lose much of the natural action. Yet, I have endured thirty years of critics saying "tricksy camera work", when I've hardly ever moved the camera. Putting them against clean backgrounds makes it so much easier for an audience to observe the body language...and body language is part of them, part of the jokes, part of the acting.'

Walter Shenson stated that Alun Owen's directive as the writer of The Beatles' debut movie was **"to create characters for them that reflect their own."** He further explained: **"We want to put over their non-conformist, slightly anarchist characters. We want to present their almost Goon-like quality."**

As the Fab Four charged through *A Hard Day's Night* precisely how much of the persona up there on the screen was of their own making and how much was the creation of first Alun Owen and then director Richard Lester is often to debate.

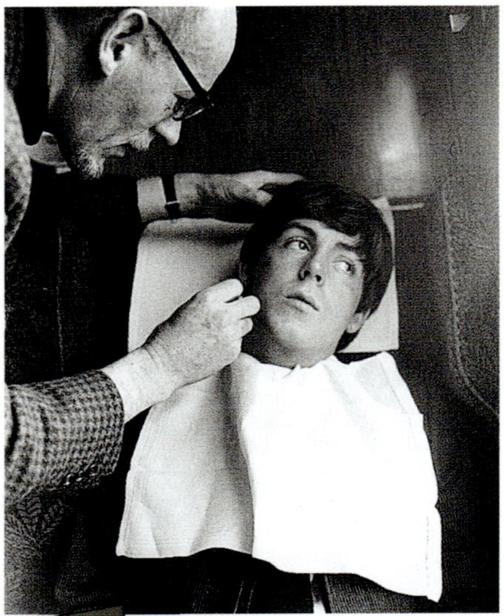

ABOVE A sketch of the original costume idea for Isla Blair in *'A Hard Day's Night'.*

TOP RIGHT A publicity still showing the scene featuring Isla Blair.

Richard Lester

'When we started on *A Hard Day's Night* the importance of separating out The Beatles' individual personalities was something which we deliberately concentrated on, and particularly so later when we got around to *Help!*...we made jokes about them being separate people and gave them each a false persona just to do that. I think that was of enormous benefit to them.'

'It was important that we gave each one of them a separate scene. We only cut Paul's out because it worked the least well. And, it was the longest. It was a scene with an actress in 18th-century costume in a rehearsal room who slowly takes bits off and isn't what she seems...it was a play on the I-am-not-really-what-I-seem-to-be. Paul did it as well as the others did theirs. At that time, he was probably the most self-conscious actor because he knew more about acting than the others. He had a girlfriend who was an actress (Jane Asher) and he was a regular visitor to the theatre. He had more to lose because he had probably thought about it a bit more.'

Paul McCartney

'To give you an example, there was a sequence that I was going to do...and, to this day, whenever I go past the pub in Shepherds Bush - on the corner by the old BBC TV Theatre - I remember going in with Isla Blair and filming on the second floor. (The Jack Billings School of Dancing). She was suppose to be the object of my desire or I was of hers...that was the idea behind this little scene-ette. I had to sort of wander around her with the camera going round and round in circles...all very Sixties, all very French and I had to repeat these very quirky lines. We had a whole day of doing that, but it didn't work because it wasn't the kind of thing we would have done in every day life...it was all a little bit too contrived.'

On the set of *A Hard Day's Night* the Beatles proved to be infinitely more attentive and co-operative than when the same team got around to filming *Help!* the following year. Lester agrees that *A Hard Day's Night* was made on pills while *Help!* was made on pot.

Richard Lester

'They hadn't fully realised just how boring film-making is. It was still fun on the set of *A Hard Day's Night*...being in control of a big toy in a way. Actually, they weren't in control because they were doing exactly as they were told. There were no real ad-libs...every word is in the script. The same with *Help!*'

'Later on, the same thing applied when I made *How I Won The War* with John. At one point while we were making that movie, I turned to John and said, "if you really wanted to, you could be a good serious or comic actor" and his reply was, "I know I probably could but, what a silly thing to do!" And there we were only into the first week of shooting, and I'm thinking to myself, "God, if he thinks it's silly how on earth am I going to get through the schedule?"'

On Monday 2 March, the cameras rolled for the first time. Paddington station was the scene of the first six days' filming at a cost of £600 a day for a train. The guard's whistle blew at 8.30 am and the train pulled out from platform five leaving behind scenes of fan mania as it chugged towards the West Country and locations such as Minehead, Taunton and Newton Abbot.

ABOVE The Danish version of the single *'A Hard Day's Night'.*

BELOW LEFT Having just checked out the British Rail menu, George does a runner.

BELOW George leaves poor Ringo and John waiting at the station.

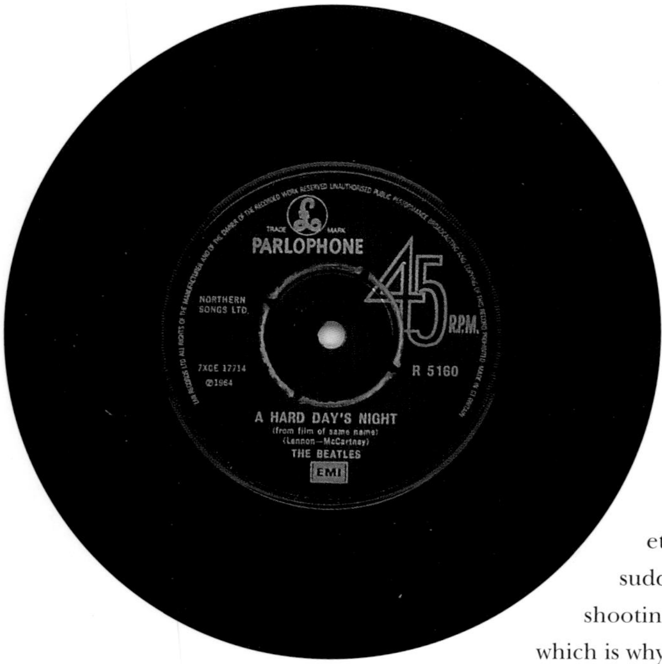

Within minutes it became apparent that this was far from a normal production. So much so that the person in charge of script continuity dashed off a memo to Lester in which she voiced her concern. Not only was she alarmed at Lester using a hand-held camera, but that The Beatles came onto the train wearing their own turtle neck sweaters , street clothes and smoking. She further bemoaned that if this was indicative of how the production was headed, **"I don't think I'm going to last the week."**

There wasn't sufficient time to stop and ponder on production etiquette. At one point, Lester directed the cameras at a mob of girls who suddenly surrounded The Beatles' limo following an exhaustive day's shooting. This clip was woven into the film - after the Beatles are in the station, which is why the group is wearing one set of clothes on the train and another while in the car.

Paddington station itself was never again used for filming. For the remainder of the railway sequences, they boarded the train at Acton. In an effort to avoid all kinds of problems created by hysterical fans, the opening sequence of *A Hard Day's Night* was in fact shot on two consecutive Sundays (5 and 12 April) at nearby Marylebone. From 10 March onwards filming took place in and around Twickenham Studios save for excursions to Les Ambassadeurs - a private night club and a mimed three-song slot for the TV programme *Ready, Steady Go* (Friday, 20 March). From 23 March to 2 April, the concert sequences were shot at the Scala Playhouse. The production team wrapped it up on Friday, 24 April.

By now, all hell was breaking loose as, almost daily, the press printed banner headline stories - many of them completely invented - which implied that The Beatles were about to break up, one (or all) of them was dying of a 'mysterious' disease, they were about to have their hair cut! Not even those with vested interests seemed fully aware of the true magnitude of Beatlemania, so that the rules were constantly being made up and revised (almost hourly) as it gained worldwide momentum. Record sales projections were useless as they all vastly underestimated growing consumer demand.

At one point during the making of *A Hard Day's Night* visiting US executives tried to persuade Lester into wiping The Beatles' voices from off the soundtrack and re-dubbing it with mid-Atlantic voices supplied by professional actors. Lester was furious and stood his ground.

Paul McCartney

'Well these were the kind of things that happened that we never heard about, but I do remember that particular incident very clearly. We said, "look if we can understand a fuckin' cowboy talking Texan they can understand us talkin' Liverpool." Anyway, we were convinced that our fans could understand us, it was just the older people that didn't try.'

Colonel Tom Parker, a slippery customer whose credo appeared to be why-sell-something-once - when-you-can-sell-it-three-times-over-to-the-same-person (and then have them thank you!), viewed the meteoric rise of these four 'foreign' intruders with a combination of amazement and envy. Sure, The Colonel and Elvis sent personal greetings and words of encouragement to The Beatles, but later, when Elvis began to lose his grip on the public, it's alleged that the pair of them personally lobbied high-ranking Government officials pointing out just how bad an influence these Beatles were on (impressionable) young Americans.

Initially, United Artists had scheduled a first run of 500,000 soundtrack albums to qualify immediately for RIAA Gold disc status. However, New York radio station WMCA triggered coast-to-coast retailer response when it previewed the soundtrack on Thursday, 25 June - a full ten days ahead of the official release. By the Monday, re-orders had pushed the figure to well over one million. In turn, that figure quickly doubled to where advance orders of two-million-and-counting made the soundtrack of *A Hard Day's Night*, potentially, the biggest-ever selling LP to date.

To say that everyone was ecstatic would be to underestimate the euphoria. United Artists Pictures' Executive Vice President Arnold Picker revealed that normally most soundtrack albums don't start to do noticeable business at the check-out until a few weeks after a movie has gone on general release and 'after the score has a chance to catch on.' What was currently unfolding was a unique situation. The final print for *A Hard Day's Night* had yet to be released by the laboratory and the upcoming soundtrack was not only guaranteed the top slot on the charts but the entire production had already clawed back its £200,000 budget and gone into profit. In actual fact, Richard Lester brought the completed film in £20,000 under budget.

Well before its premiere, demand for a *A Hard Day's Night* resulted in the then unprecedented world wide order of between 1,500 and 1,800 prints of the movie. The United States alone accounted for 700 prints while the UK took a minimum of 110. In Germany, the count was 70.

United Artists informed the media that, during the August-September period, *A Hard Day's Night* would be playing on a saturation basis in every available market around the globe, with 'more prints in circulation than for any other pic in history.'

A Hard Day's Night went on general release on 12 August in the States. However, before then, United Artists revealed that they had raked in well over half-a-million dollars alone from special previews and premieres. As interest intensified, more than 100 cities across the United States requested the movie before its official release date and over 150,000 tickets were pre-sold for these premieres. UA anticipated a one million box office gross in the UK. Just about everyone succumbed to *A Hard Day's Night*.

ABOVE The ticket for the Royal World premiere of *'A Hard Day's Night'*, in London.

ABOVE The Fab Four arrive in style for the premiere of *'A Hard Day's Night'.*

at-our-elbows instead of looking at the film... you just keep looking at the back of your elbow as though you've never seen it before! The fact was, we really were a bit surprised and it was not quite what we thought when we looked at it earlier in a preview, but once we got to the premiere...which was this really huge event with thousands of people everywhere...and heard people laughing and heard people appreciating it, I think we were all pretty well sold by then.'

London's West End had never before experienced a movie premiere quite like that for *A Hard Day's Night* which took place at the London Pavilion and which coincided with Ringo's 24th birthday (15 guinea's for VIP seats). Over 20,000 hysterical Beatles fans crammed into Piccadilly Circus and the adjoining streets. Local restaurateurs insisted they hadn't witnessed crowds like these since V-E Night, 19 years earlier. While 200 policemen tried to manage the scenes of mayhem, a team of ambulance men, nurses and doctors attended to 100 fans who'd fainted.

Princess Margaret, accompanied by her then husband Lord Snowdon, quizzed Paul what he thought of their screen debut. He answered; **"I don't think we are very good, ma'am, but we had a very good producer and director."** To which the Princess confided. **"You have nothing to worry about, it was fine."** When the Princess enquired after George what the expression that shirt is grotty meant George replied; **"Grotty is the current slang word for grotesque."**

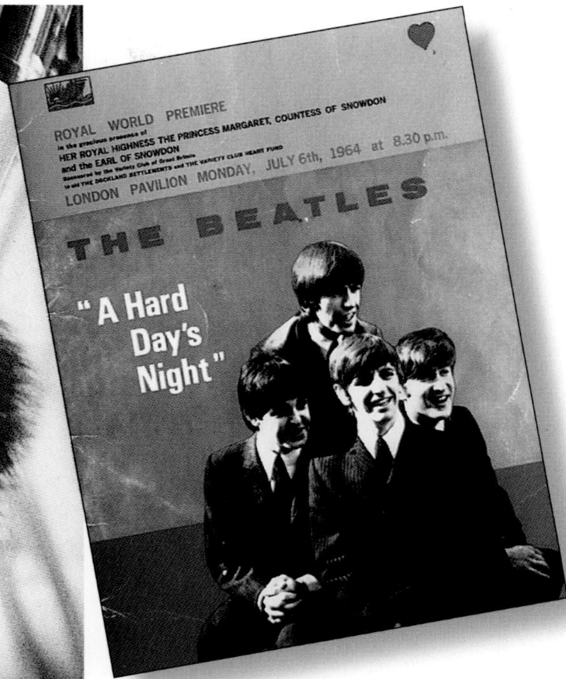

Later that evening, The Beatles discussed the current state of play with two of their party guests, Rolling Stones' Keith Richards and Brian Jones.

Paul McCartney

'The cash is the big change and the cash changes you. But, it can't change you inside because to go big-headed you've got to be big-headed anyway. We think we've got something, because we'd be idiots if we didn't. The danger is in narrow-minded people, soft people, who will say, "Ah it's gone to their heads and they're big-headed."'

John was more down to earth and quite obviously had something on his mind!

ABOVE Ringo receives a quick wash and brush up.

ABOVE The Fab Four flanked by their on-screen roadies, Shake (John Junkin) and Norm (Norman Rossington).

John Lennon
'In another year I'll have me money and I'll be out of it.'

George Harrison
'When this job finishes, we actors will be out of work!'

Did working with professional actors on the set of *A Hard Day's Night* amount to trial-by-ordeal or did they find the cast genuinely helpful and compassionate?

Paul McCartney
'Look, we were just a bunch of kids down from Liverpool and we were quite taken with them all. Norman Rossington was a Liverpool lad and so very downhome and good streetwise, and John Junkin who played his mate was genuinely funny - and still is. Victor (Spinetti) was lovely and is still a friend. Even the old man on the train - Richard Vernon, he was very lovely guy as well. Fortunately, we got on extremely well with all the people who were in it.'

'Wilfred Brambell (who played Paul's cantankerous grandfather) was great...the only terrible thing for us was that Wilfred kept forgetting his lines. And, we couldn't believe it. See, we expected all the actors to be very professional and word perfect - couldn't imagine that an actor like Wilfred could ever do a thing like...forget his lines! So, we were very shocked and embarrassed by this.'

Richard Lester has spoken about how co-operative and professional all four Fabs were during the shooting.

Paul McCartney
'The funny thing about rock'n'roll that makes me laugh, is that people are always supposed to be hoodlums and hoods and ripping up cinemas and theatres. It was never the bands that did any ripping up - most of them were reasonable people when you scratched the surface. Truth is, it was just one or two Teds in the audience who maybe ripped up one or two seats - and that was a phase that didn't last too long. It wasn't like we were Hell's Angels, but the image was like...these guys are wacky and probably crazy and probably drink a lot or something. Actually, we were fairly average, witty lads who loved our music and were slightly anarchic, but nothing more than that.'

Ever since The Beatles had hit the big time and (understandably) moved south to London, they were constantly subjected to petty (yet still hurtful) snipes and accusations of having turned their backs on their original fans and deserting them. The Beatles themselves even began to think that maybe there was some truth in it, that success had caused them to abandon their home city. Therefore, there was much apprehension in the Beatles' camp about the reception they would receive when a Liverpool premiere for *A Hard Day's Night* was announced.

As events demonstrated, the reception that greeted them far exceeded their wildest imagination. They returned as conquering heroes. Not even a local cup winning soccer team could have expected to receive such a spontaneous homecoming. It seemed that the entire city had turned out to welcome them home. Over 150,000 people lined the 10-mile route from the airport to the city centre.

George Harrison
'After this, nothing matters. This is the ultimate.'

ABOVE An alternative US billboard poster.

At the time of its release, John Lennon concurred with Paul that *A Hard Day's Night* faithfully mirrored the time in which it was shot.

Paul McCartney
'It was a good projection of one facade of us, which was on tour, it was of us in that situation together, in a hotel, having to perform before people. We were like that.'

However, Lennon didn't disguise the fact that he felt it could have been more realistic and hard-edged. Years later, he would frequently revise his opinions of that era and almost everything else in his life to the point of contradiction.

John Lennon
'Alun Owen was a bit phoney. He was like a professional Liverpool man, like a professional American. He stayed with us for two days and wrote the whole thing based on our characters then: mine - witty, Ringo - dumb and cute, George, this, Paul, that.'

Lennon further claimed to be infuriated by the glibness of the end product and 'shittyness' of the dialogue. If, in his final assumption, about half of *A Hard Day's Night* was 'OK' Lennon felt *Help!* was 'bullshit'...though Dick Lester's comic strip Batman idea in *Help!* was ahead of its time. But by the mid-Seventies, Lennon had become quite cynical about fame;

John Lennon
'As far as things went The Beatles were that band that gigged around Liverpool, played down the Cavern, went to Hamburg. After *A Hard Day's Night* it was something entirely different. *A Hard Day's Night* is really the tail-end of things.'

The Beatles, he opined, were unrecognisable compared with how he had originally conceived them. In the wake of the hysteria that accompanied *A Hard Day's Night*, The Beatles, he insisted, were nothing other than public property.

John Lennon
'A money-making machine for everyone who could grab a piece of the action. I never imagined that it would all end up with lawyers fighting and Paul and I not speaking to each other. I mean, what the fuck was that? It was never meant to be like that! Never!! After that it was Beatles-by-numbers. Say something witty John, wear something wacky Paul, George you be strong and silent and Ringo - just be Ringo.'

A Hard Day's Night simultaneously opened in 500 cinemas and earned $1.3 million in rentals during its first week rising to $5.8-million by the end of six weeks. Added to this was one million dollars gross from their concert tour and Stateside record sales in excess of ten million. New York's prestigious *Village Voice* hailed *A Hard Day's Night* as 'the *Citizen Kane* of juke box musicals.' *Time* magazine's endorsement was as, 'One of the smoothest, freshest, funniest films ever made for the purposes of exploitation.'

Meanwhile, it was estimated that no fewer than one out of every 15 Liverpudlians between the ages of 15 and 24 were now in a beat group. In all, 350 plus groups were said to be operating on Merseyside. However, not everyone was joyful. Against a backdrop of record company asset strippers having arrived from London to all but plunder the local scene, *Mersey Beat* editor Bill Harry and a ceaseless champion of the local talent insisted, **"The rot has set in. Success has turned the scene rotten. It has sapped the energy and made a happy scene a rat race."**

A United Artists Release
Walter Shenson-Subafilms Production

Director	Richard Lester
Producer	Walter Shenson

CAST

John Lennon	*John*
Paul McCartney	*Paul*
George Harrison	*George*
Ringo Starr	*Ringo*
Wilfred Brambell	*Grandfather*
Norman Rossington	*Norm*
John Junkin	*Shake*
Victor Spinetti	*Television Director*
Kenneth Haigh	*Shirt Advertising Man*
Anna Quayle	*Millie*
Deryck Guyler	*Police Sergeant*
Richard Vernon	*Pompous Traveller*
Michael Trubshawe	*Club Manager*
Eddie Malin	*Waiter*

and
Bridget Armstrong
Roger Avon
Lionel Blair
John Bluthal
Patti Boyd

CREDITS

Director	Richard Lester
Production Company	Proscenium Films
Producer	Walter Shenson
Associate Producer	Denis O'Dell
Assistant Director	John D. Merriman
Scriptwriter	Alun Owen
Photography	Gilbert Taylor
Editor	John Jympson
Art Director	Ray Simm
Songs	John Lennon & Paul McCartney
Music Director	George Martin
Costumes	Julie Harris
Titles	Robert Freeman
Sound Recording	H.L. Bird Stephen Dalby
Length	7650 feet (2332 metres)
Running Time	85 minutes
UK Premiere	6 July, 1964
US Premiere	12 August, 1964

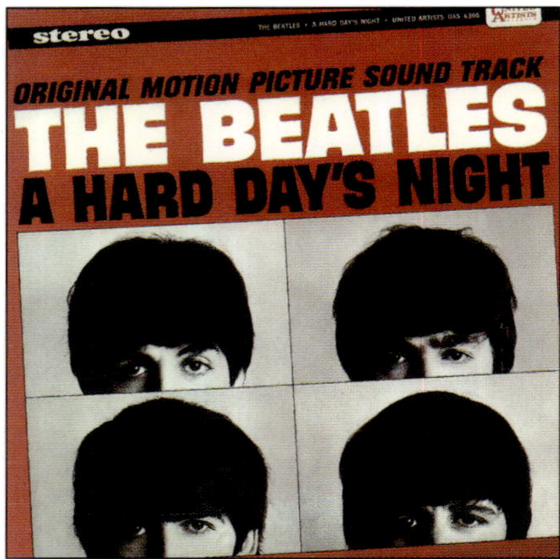

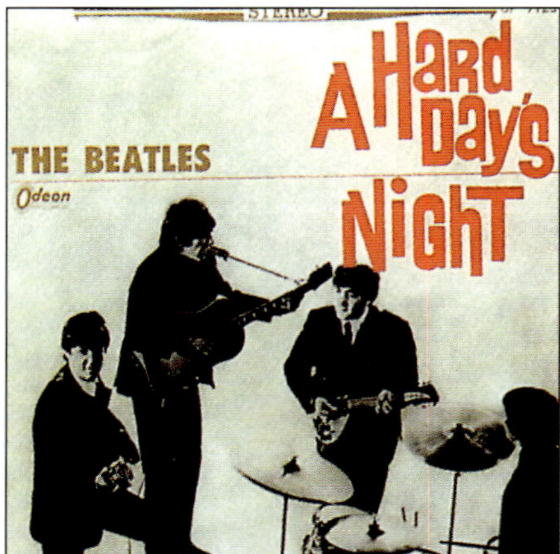

ABOVE Various LP covers for *'A Hard Day's Night'*.
TOP: US cover.
MIDDLE: Japanese cover.
BOTTOM: French cover.

A HARD DAYS NIGHT

Parlophone PMC 1230 (mono)
PCS 3058 (stereo)
Produced: George Martin
Released: 10 July, 1964

(+) *First attempt*

SIDE ONE

1 **A Hard Day's Night** (John)
Tuesday, 16 April, 1964

2 **I Should Have Known Better** (John)
(+) *Tuesday, 25 February*
Recorded Wednesday, 26 February, 1964

3 **If I Fell** (John/Paul)
Thursday, 27 February, 1964

4 **I'm Happy Just To Dance With You** (George)
Sunday, 1 March, 1964

5 **And I Love Her** (Paul)
(+) *Tuesday, 25 February*
Recorded Wednesday, 26 February & Thursday 27 February , 1964

6 **Tell Me Why** (John/Paul)
Thursday, 27 February, 1964

7 **Can't Buy Me Love** (Paul)
Wednesday, 29 January, 1964

SIDE TWO

1 **Any Time At All** (John)
Tuesday, 2 June, 1964

2 **I'll Cry Instead** (John/Paul)
Monday, 1 June, 1964

3 **Things We Said Today** (Paul)
Tuesday, 2 June, 1964

4 **When I Get Home** (John)
Tuesday, 2 June, 1964

5 **You Can't Do That** (John)
dropped from final soundtrack
Tuesday, 25 February, 1964

6 **I'll Be Back** (John)
Monday, 1 June, 1964

US VERSION

United Artists UA 6366 (mono)
UAS 6366 (stereo)
Released: 26 June, 1964

SIDE ONE

1 **A Hard Day's Night**
2 **Tell Me Why**
3 **I'll Cry Instead**
(mistitled **'I Cry Instead'**)
4 **I Should Have Known Better** (instrumental)*
5 **I'm Happy Just To Dance With You**
6 **And I Love Her** (instrumental)*

SIDE TWO

1 **I Should Have Known Better**
2 **If I Fell**
3 **And I Love Her**
4 **Ringo's Theme *(This Boy)*** (instrumental)*
5 **Can't Buy Me Love**
6 **A Hard Day's Night** (instrumental)*

(*) The George Martin Orchestra

UK 45s

A: **Can't Buy Me Love**
B: **You Can't Do That**
Parlophone R5114
Released: 20 March, 1964

A: **A Hard Day's Night**
B: **Things We Said Today**
Parlophone R5160
Released: 10 July, 1964

US 45s

A: **Can't Buy Me Love**
B: **You Can't Do That**
Capitol 5150
Released: 16 March, 1964

A: **A Hard Day's Night**
B: **I Should Have Known Better**
Capitol 5222
Released: 13 July, 1964

A: **I'll Cry Instead**
B: **I'm Happy Just To Dance With You**
Capitol 5234
Released: 20 July, 1964

A: **And I Love Her**
B: **If I Fell**
Capitol 5235
Released: 20 July, 1964

UK EPs

Extracts From The Film 'A Hard Day's Night'
Parlophone GEP 8920
Released: 6 November, 1964
A: **I Should Have Known Better**
If I Fell
B: **Tell Me Why**
And I Love Her

Extracts From The Film 'A Hard Day's Night'
Parlophone GEP 8924
Released: 6 November, 1964
A: **Any Time At All**
I'll Cry Instead
B: **Things We Said Today**
When I Get Home

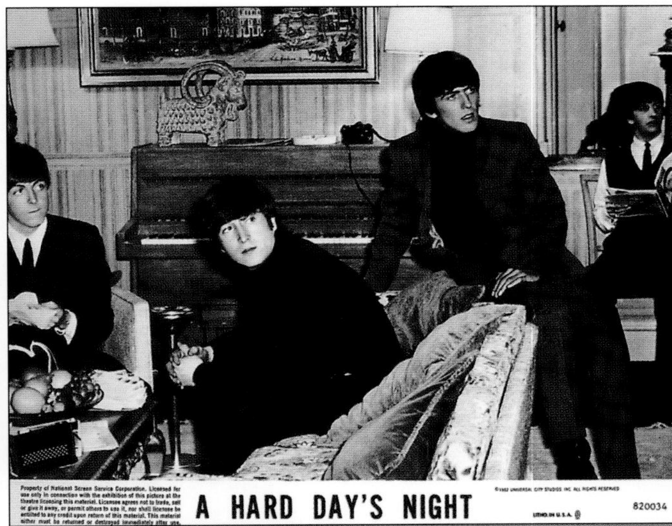

ABOVE Various different publicity press cards showing various scenes from the film *'A Hard Day's Night'*.

<u>**Production note:**</u>
At the same Paris recording sessions that produced *'Can't Buy Me Love'* (Wednesday, 29 January, 1964) German language vocals were dubbed onto the existing instrumental tracks for **'Komm, Gib Mir Deine Hand' ('I Want To Hold Your Hand')** and **'Sie Liebt Dich' ('She Loves You')**.

Other material recorded at Abbey Road during later sessions for *'A Hard Day's Night'* included:

I Call Your Name (John)
Sunday, 1 March, 1964
was dropped from soundtrack

Long Tall Sally (Paul)
Sunday, 1 March, 1964

Matchbox (Ringo)
Monday, 1 June, 1964

Slow Down (John)
Monday, 1 June, 1964

All four titles would comprise a 19 June, 1964 EP release **'Long Tall Sally'** Parlophone GEP 8913 (mono)

6

HELP!

'I don't mind colour in a film if it doesn't mean dancing about in a red shirt, like in one of Cliff's. I don't like that.'
George Harrison (May 1965)

On the 30th October 1965, it was announced that The Beatles next feature length movie - their second - would be a comedy thriller. The screenplay, for this as yet untitled vehicle, was being written by Mark Behm whose previous credits included the original storyline for Audrey Hepburn's comedy-thriller *Charade*. The Beatles, it was claimed, were being given the opportunity to assist Behm with the script and John and Paul would then shape it into The Beatles idiom. This way they would have the chance to put their own phrases into the finished script, **"in order to get the kind of things they say in real life into it."**

George Harrison
'We'll be making another film in February, but I've no idea what it'll be all about. I hope there are no songs in it. It was all right getting songs in the last one because we had an excuse, they worked into the film all right. But I don't like these films where everybody bursts into song for no reason and you have a full orchestra blasting out from nowhere. Yes, I'd prefer to make a film without any singing.'

A production budget of £500,000 (approximately one million dollars and twice the cost of *A Hard Day's Night*), had been set aside for this new venture. On the strength of his success with *A Hard Day's Night*, Richard Lester's fee, as Director, had also been increased to a respectable figure approaching £30,000. Producer Walter Shenson informed everyone within earshot: **"The film will be a mad, zany comedy thriller and definitely not like the first film. No other casting has been made - but it will all fall into place when we start. The boys are pretty good at this sort of thing."**

ABOVE The UK billboard poster for the film.

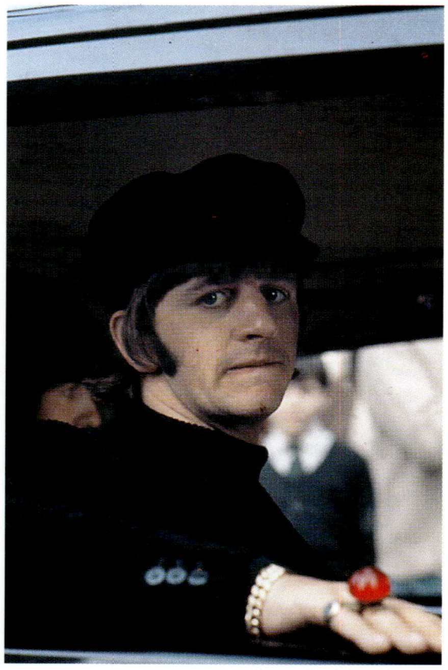

ABOVE Ringo showing off his ring that is the centre of attention for the film *'Help!'*.

The Beatles were expected to record up to ten new songs from which around half a dozen would be selected for the soundtrack. In actual fact, they produced a total of 14. Paul revealed that neither he nor John consulted the script before embarking upon recording potential soundtrack material.

Paul McCartney
'We just write songs and they are fitted into the film. That's what we did last time. We're not like other songwriters who get suggestions from certain lines in a script. Often we write tunes first without having a title. We'll get that later. But a lot of people work like that.'

Richard Lester
'As with *A Hard Day's Night*, they gave me around nine songs and I picked out seven, It wasn't a case of me not liking the other songs and making a critical judgement - that is something I never did. I just looked at the tempos and what images I thought I could put with them.'

Aside from a handful of journalists that they had befriended earlier, The Beatles had now become highly suspicious of the Press at large. Not without reason. Stories were constantly fabricated: Ringo seriously ill, The Beatles to split, The Beatles on the slide, a bad example to young people. Their collective response was 'We never said we were symbols of British youth. Other people said that. We are just a rock 'n' roll group playing the music we like. Getting well paid for it. And so what?'

Much was made of the fact that the second Beatles' movie went into production without a title, being referred to by both crew and cast as 'Beatles 2'. What wasn't known was that the actual plot had undergone a drastic overhaul before finally emerging as the familiar yarn centred around the thuggish cult followers of the Goddesss Kaili frantically pursuing The Beatles up the Austrian Alps, across Salisbury Plain and along the beaches of the Bahamas in an effort to retrieve a sacred ring worn by Ringo. As would be expected, all attempts to remove this religious artefact from Ringo's finger are thwarted. Neither was it revealed, that, originally it was perceived as a possible vehicle for Peter Sellers.

Before the film was put into production, Lester had developed a growth on his forehead which required prompt medical attention. The day he had it surgically removed under a local anaesthetic was also the same day he was to meet up with Paul McCartney at Annabel's in London's fashionable West End to explain the original plot for 'Beatles 2'. When evening came, Lester, still not fully recovered from his ordeal and with his bandages dripping blood, stumbled into this exclusive London night club somewhat dazed.

ABOVE Paul and John accidentally find themselves in a fashion shoot for the latest in heavy cable knitwear.

Richard Lester

'As it turned out, I accidentally discovered that the plot that I had invented was also the very same as one being filmed elsewhere at that very time. It was Jean Paul Belmondo's sequel *Les Tribulations d'un Chinoise en Chine* to his very successful *That Man From Rio*. The plot to my story had Ringo complaining that he could no longer cope with his stressed-filled life. Anyway, there he is in this bar complaining "I can't go on anymore" when the person sitting right next to him says, "if you haven't got the courage to put an end to it yourself, I'll do it for you at a price. I'm a professional assassin". So Ringo agrees and gives him a cheque only to wake up the following morning realising what a dreadful mistake he's made and panics. The rest of the plot is obvious. As things turned out, because of the similarity to the film Belmondo was making, we had to change The Beatles' script somewhat.'

'Apart from that problem, what I didn't want to do was another fictional documentary - but, this time in colour. Neither did I want to cast them in something like the *Three Musketeers*, because nobody would have taken them seriously. Whatever the second film was going to be, we had to make certain that they still played themselves, but what we didn't want to do is what we did with *A Hard Day's Night* - show them at work. I couldn't show what they did at play because that would have been X-rated, so I had to make them passive and attach a plot onto them that was silly enough that nobody would take it seriously.'

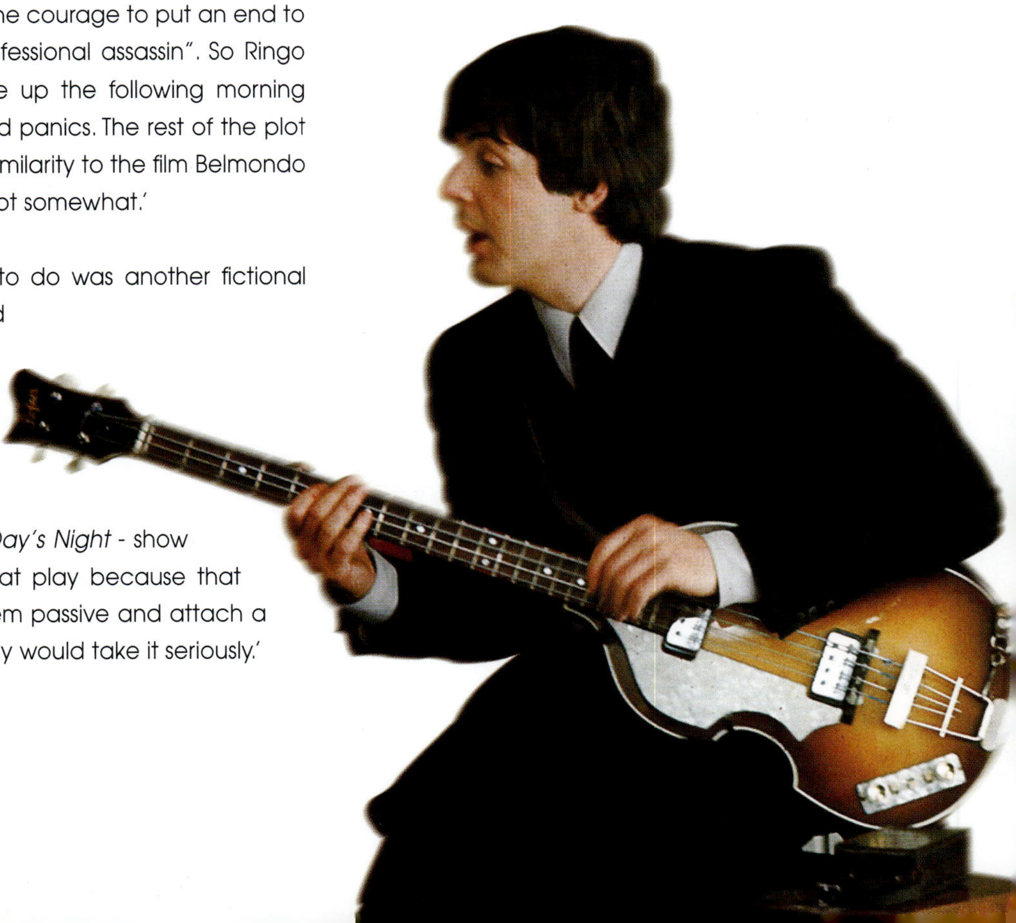

In between *A Hard Day's Night* and *Help!*, the Beatles kept themselves busy. Apart from the seemingly endless string of one-nighters, radio broadcasts and television appearances they squeezed in a world tour that embraced Denmark, the Netherlands, Hong Kong, Australia, New Zealand and Sweden, returned to the States (August-September), rampaged around the UK (October-November), released a new album 'Beatles For Sale' and undertook a 20-night run of 'Another Beatles Christmas Show' in London (December - January).

Elsewhere, Richard Lester directed the comedy *The Knack* which starred Rita Tushingham, Ray Brooks, Michael Crawford and Donal Donnelly and, scooped the major prize at the prestigious Cannes Film Festival. Based on the play by Ann Jellicoe, the screenplay for *The Knack* had been written by Charles Wood. And it was Wood who was hired to prepare the screenplay of what was eventually to become *Help!*

Wood hadn't been introduced to The Beatles at the time, apparently, learning all he needed to know about the Fab Four from repeated screenings of *A Hard Day's Night*. Said Wood: **"Really, they're just lads who have a talent for presenting themselves."** This time around, they didn't get as much opportunity in *Help!* to be themselves as they had in their screen debut. In part, this was due to the fact that they had been supplied with a fictitious comic-strip storyline and dialogue that was extremely tight. Said Wood, **"They've handled my dialogue seriously but they must treat their acting as a bit of a farce - this is the only way of doing their best."** He added that when the Beatles were fooling around, in reality, **"they're really working their hardest."** Charles Wood, so it appears was quite disappointed, that in the final run-up to its release, *Help!* replaced the original 'Beatles 2' working title. **"They should have kept it as it was!"**

The Beatles may have been a small phenomenon when they started *A Hard Day's Night* but by the time *Help!* went into production, they were unquestionably the biggest act in the world. A fact not lost on United Artists.

ABOVE Poster showing the billing for 'Another Beatles Christmas show'.

TOP John picks a winner.

If Richard Lester's fast moving a-day-in-the-life 'film-journalism' approach to *A Hard Day's Night* had achieved its purpose of separating out The Beatles' individual personalities, *Help!* and any successive movies would have to adhere to an entirely new game plan. Aware of the fickle nature of pop, Walter Shenson didn't shy away from the fact that *Help!* was far more crucial to their future business plan than *A Hard Day's Night* had ever been. While flattered by the comparisons, United Artists attempted to play down numerous press stories that constantly likened The Beatles to former movie comedy team the Marx Brothers.

Yet, behind closed doors, there had been serious discussions of how best to fuse the surreal Goon-like humour that had worked so well in *A Hard Day's Night* to the unique style of snappy wise-cracking foolery that had made the Marx Brothers such a tremendous box office hit. And while Richard Lester's direction had been nothing less than innovative, storywise, those who controlled the budgets also agreed that they should be mindful that basic plots should never stray too far away from the money-making mainstream.

Walter Shenson

'There is no question of The Beatles playing anything but the Beatles, but the pop market is a teenage market and, by its standards, the boys have had a fantastically long run, and nobody can expect it to go on for ever. But I've no doubt they can establish themselves as great screen personalities.'

As a means of protecting United Artists' investment, The Beatles would no longer be expected to carry a film almost entirely on their own. For *Help!* a highly experienced team of comic actors, led by Leo McKern and including Victor Spinetti, Eleanor Bron, Bruce Lacey, Patrick Cargill and John Bluthal, was hired not to appear in 'cameo', but to play an integral part of the plot from start to finish.

ABOVE An Italian billboard poster advertising *'Help!'*.

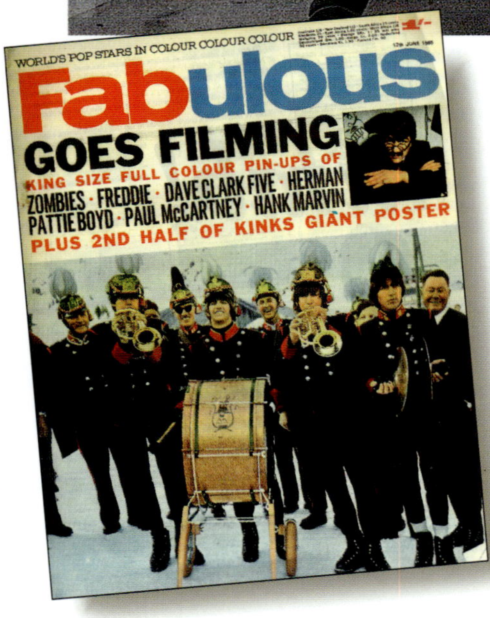

John Lennon

'*Help!* was a drag because we didn't know what was happening. In fact, Richard Lester was a bit ahead of his time with the Batman thing but we were on pot by then and all the best stuff is on the cutting room floor, with us breaking up and falling all over the place.'

In keeping with procedures adopted by most studios, almost all the *Help!* out-takes - including an entire sequence with comedian Frankie Howerd - were destroyed after one year to facilitate storage problems.

According to Lester, Lennon wasn't far from the truth when he commented, that The Beatles became extras in their own film.

Richard Lester

'It was because they were put up against professional actors who were saying these bizarre lines better than they did. The Beatles made no real attempt at them because they were stoned throughout and probably thought "oh, sod this." The Beatles used pot as a continuing device to amuse themselves because film-making didn't amuse them any longer. We had some wonderful times, but it had all become a bit of a giggle. The novelty of being around a film crew had obviously worn off and pot was there to alleviate the boredom of hanging around between takes.'

TOP Eleanor Bron hanging out with the lads between takes.

Due to the unprecedented success of *A Hard Day's Night*, the budgets for *Help!* had been increased considerably. The schedule stated that the film would go into production on 23 February and that all filming had to be completed by 12 May. Furthermore, it had been agreed that a sizable part of the film would be shot in the Bahamas, where it was hoped to set up a company which would provide a shelter against British taxes.

Paul McCartney
'When we began discussing where we were going to film, we said, "can we go away somewhere exotic for this one...like can you write a scene set in the Bahamas?" Then the lawyers thought "aha, we'll tie that in with tax dodges" which didn't work of course. A guy called Walter Strach spent about a year in a house we were supposed to have bought in the Bahamas. Then, one day, he said, "sorry I've sold the house you can't go there", it doesn't really work. It was a little bit of a scam that way.'

The Beatles returned to Britain on 11 March, suitably sun-tanned, affording them just sufficient time to swap their tropical casual wear for appropriate winter thermals for a hectic six day Austrian sojourn (14-20 March) to film their memorable 'Ticket To Ride' sequence on the ski slopes around Obertauern.

Once this part of the shooting schedule was completed, almost all of the remaining filming took place in and around the Twickenham Studios, save for going on location to Salisbury Plain (3-5 May), where, surrounded by a real-life division of fighting units and a troop of horse artillery, they pretended to record 'I Need You'.

ABOVE Ringo up to his knees in the Bahamas on the cover of the Observer Sunday magazine, April 1965.

LEFT Paul shows off a local souvenir to the envy of the others.

Other than Ringo's riverside walkabout and their own frantic running, jumping and standing still sequence to the accompaniment of 'Can't Buy Me Love', the most memorable scenes in *A Hard Day's Night*, remain the surrealistic events in the bathroom and the brief backstage encounter between John and Anna Quayle. In *Help!*, along with the 'Ticket To Ride' episode in the Alps, the one scene that sticks is an inventive Richard Lester sight-gag that occurs close to the beginning of the film.

John, Paul, George and Ringo, returning home, stroll up the paths of their respective terraced houses (in Ailsa Avenue, Twickenham) watched by two middle-aged women. As they are about to open their red, green, orange and blue front doors simultaneously, their neighbours wave and remark: **"Lovely lads, and so natural. I mean, adoration has not gone to their heads one jot, has it? You know what I mean - success?...still the same as they were before...not spoilt one bit, just ordinary lads."** They then step from what, outside looks like a two-up/two-down, into a fantasy world in the form of a vast and palatially furnished communal room, stocked with all manner of state-of-the-art gadgetry, automatic machines and John Lennon's sunken bed.

Now back to that title! En route from the Bahamas to Saltzburg, The Beatles explained their predicament.

George Harrison
'We had a couple of ideas, but they just didn't click. It's got to be a title that all four of us will click our fingers at, and say, "This is it!" Like *A Hard Day's Night* we knew straight away that was the title we wanted.'

Paul McCartney
'It's maddening. We must come up with something soon - and it's got to be funny. George is losing his hair with worry over it!'

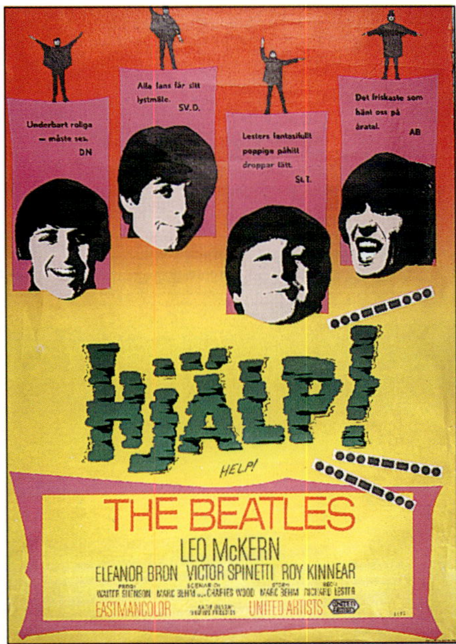

ABOVE Swedish billboard poster for the film *'Help!'*.

TOP RIGHT Having mislaid his drum kit, Ringo quickly improvises.

Suddenly, a title 'Eight Arms To Hold You' (yet another suggestion from Ringo) began appearing in print. And, in much the same way as 'I'll Cry Instead' inadvertently ended up on the US version of the *A Hard Day's Night* soundtrack album, the Stateside part of the operation again jumped the gun, so the initial pressing of 'Ticket To Ride' (on Capitol) had from the United Artists' release *'Eight Arms To Hold You'* emblazoned on the label. But then, back home even The Beatles were still under the illusion that this was the agreed title.

Richard Lester

'We then realised that it would be bloody difficult for them to write a song around that title. I had originally wanted the script to be called *Help, Help*, but was informed that such a title had already been registered with the Writers' Guild Of America. "

Lester was advised by a lawyer that, legally, he could get around this predicament if only by the fact of placing an exclamation mark at the end of it.

Richard Lester

'So, I said "sod this, it's going to be *Help!*"...this was around the second week in April and only three weeks before we finished shooting. Within thirty hours, The Beatles had written and recorded 'Help!'. Apparently, they wrote most of it in the back of the car on the way home from the studio.'

ABOVE A couple of Mexican billboard posters.

RIGHT Scotland Yard's finest give The Beatles a display of modern police tactics.

ABOVE A rare poster showing a disgruntled and diminished Paul, from one of the scenes in *'Help!'*.

LEFT John wildly impressed by Paul's piano artistry.

ABOVE The British downhill racing team - not!

OPPOSITE PAGE Yet another attempted image make-over for the lads.

Lennon later referred to 'Help!' (along with 'Strawberry Fields Forever' and 'You've Got To Hide Your Love Away') as one of his "true songs" the ones he wrote from experience.

John Lennon

'...and not projecting myself into a situation and writing a nice story about it which I always found phoney. I would try to express what I felt about myself, which I'd done in my books. Because I meant it, it's real. The lyric is as good now as it was then...It makes me feel secure to know that I was that sensible, or whatever, not sensible, but aware of myself then. It was just me singing 'Help!' and I meant it. I don't like the recording that much, the song I like. We did it too fast, to try to be commercial.'

Paul McCartney concurs with John Lennon's remarks that whereas *A Hard Day's Night* was fuelled by pills, the making of *Help!* was assisted by the communal use of aromatic herbs. And, accordingly, this second movie was somewhat vague.

Paul McCartney

'A lot more vague...but looking back on it, *Help!* isn't such a bad film. It's more of a fun romp, but I think that *A Hard Day's Night* is the better of

RM

the two. By the time we flew out to the Bahamas, it wasn't a case of George saying, he'd forgotten the script. I think what Richard meant was that he hadn't read it. But there were some interesting moments in it for all of us...going skiing was good fun and we got some nice ad libs out of that. Ringo falling down-hill was genuine. They just happened to have the cameras rolling at the time. That was Ringo learning to ski! Mind you, they told us at the time...whatever you do, don't ski...just stand there because the insurance doesn't cover any of you skiing. So of course we skied and tried to learn how to do it. But it was in colour...and this time it had a storyline, though I don't think as good a script as the first one. We weren't actually entranced by it, but it was OK.'

Richard Lester

'The sequence of them learning to ski in the Austrian Alps just fell together naturally against them singing 'Ticket To Ride'. I'd discussed this with my editor...told him that I had my own ideas, but said, "here's the material, just put anything in any order that you think works!" Anyway, he edited it all together in one go and we only had to change about three edits from a total of 150. It all just fell into something truly wonderful. It was, without doubt, one of the best things in the entire movie.'

Their eighth consecutive Number One, 'Ticket To Ride', was released on 9 April 1965, while The Beatles were still down at Twickenham Studios busily filming. This was two days before they took a break to perform a teaser for their upcoming film (plus four other songs) during the *New Musical Express* 1964-65 Annual Readers' Poll Winners' Concert staged at Wembley in the afternoon. That same evening they also made a live appearance on *The Eamonn Andrews Show.*

George Harrison

'We are always worried with each record. With 'Ticket To Ride' we were even more worried. There's bound to be a time when we come in at 19. But this Number One business doesn't seem to stop - great while it lasts, but now we'll have to start all over again and people will start predicting funny things for the next one.'

Ringo Starr

'I'm glad it's top - quite honestly I didn't expect it. Of course it makes it even more difficult for the next single. The knockers can't have a go at us just yet but I suppose their day is bound to come eventually. It's got to stop somewhere hasn't it?'

ABOVE The Beatles opt for matching sports models.

On the eve of the release of *Help!* Richard Lester admitted to the press; **"You'll find nothing new about *Help!*. There's not one bit of insight into a social phenomenon of our times. It's a comic-strip adventure; one long chase with Oriental church leaders who want to fill their temples with sacrifices and mad scientists who want to blow up the world."** Precisely. It's a story of middle-Eastern violence and intrigue that still sounds all-too-familiar in these much-troubled times. Aware that the public still wanted to see the Beatles portraying their lovable moptop selves, Lester elaborated; **"Now they are family entertainers rather that pop stars in transition."**

Lester who claimed to be a born pessimist, was aware that the public's initial romance with The Beatles was not so intense as it had been the previous year when *A Hard Day's Night* first hit the world's screens to the accompaniment of unprecedented hysteria. **"Also, though the boys are still playing themselves, this film is the test to see whether they can go any farther, play other characters. It's a transition in their career."** Secretly, Lester was aware that perhaps this was the limit, but was prepared to direct them again, though he would reverse that opinion with the release of *How I Won The War*. **"I'd be jealous of anybody else who directed them. Their pictures are such a marvellous opportunity to enjoy yourself. What I've always wanted to communicate in my work is exuberance because I enjoy it so much myself. It's the great quality that The Beatles have."**

'Help!' was the first album to ever have a pre-release order of over one million in the USA. In total, fourteen tracks were originally recorded for soundtrack consideration.

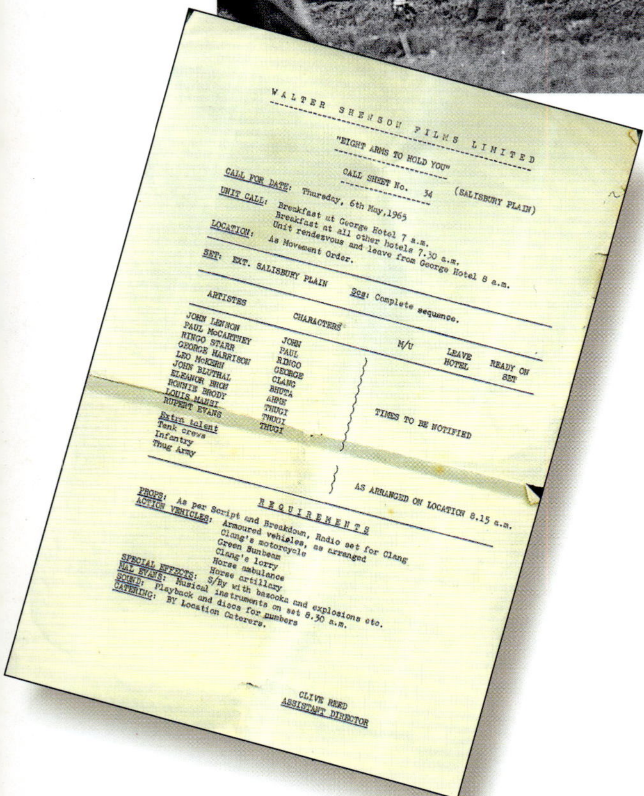

WALTER SHENSON FILMS LIMITED

"EIGHT ARMS TO HOLD YOU"

CALL SHEET No. 34 (SALISBURY PLAIN)

CALL FOR DATE: Thursday, 6th May, 1965

UNIT CALL: Breakfast at George Hotel 7 a.m.
Breakfast at all other hotels 7.30 a.m.
Unit rendezvous and leave from George Hotel 8 a.m.

LOCATION: As Movement Order.

SET: EXT. SALISBURY PLAIN Sc: Complete sequence.

ARTISTES	CHARACTERS	M/U	LEAVE HOTEL	READY ON SET
JOHN LENNON	JOHN			
PAUL McCARTNEY	PAUL			
RINGO STARR	RINGO			
GEORGE HARRISON	GEORGE			
LEO McKERN	CLANG			
JOHN BLUTHAL	BHUTA			
ELEANOR BRON	AHME	TIMES TO BE NOTIFIED		
RONNIE BRODY	THUGI			
LOUIS MANSI	THUGI			
RUPERT EVANS	THUGI			
Extra talent				
Tank crews				
Infantry				
Thug Army				
		AS ARRANGED ON LOCATION 8.15 a.m.		

REQUIREMENTS

PROPS: As per Script and Breakdown, Radio set for Clang
ACTION VEHICLES: Armoured vehicles, as arranged
Clang's motorcycle
Green Sunbeam
Clang's lorry
Horse ambulance
Horse artillery
SPECIAL EFFECTS: S/By with bazooka and explosions etc.
MAL EVANS: Musical instruments on set 8.30 a.m.
SOUND: Playback and discs for numbers
CATERING: BY Location Caterers.

CLIVE REED
ASSISTANT DIRECTOR

ABOVE The 'call sheet' for the Salisbury Plain section, shot while the film was still using the title *'Eight Arms To Hold You'*.

TOP The Beatles set up in front of their latest tour bus!!

I Need You (George)
Monday, 15 February, 1965

Another Girl (Paul)
Monday, 15 February, 1965

Ticket To Ride (John)
Monday, 15 February, 1965

Yes It Is (John/Paul/George)
dropped from actual soundtrack
Monday, 15 February, 1965

The Night Before (Paul)
Wednesday, 17 February, 1965

You Like Me Too Much (George)
dropped from actual soundtrack
Wednesday, 17 February, 1965

Tell Me What You See (John/Paul)
dropped from actual soundtrack
Thursday, 18 February, 1965

You've Got To Hide Your Love Away (John)
Thursday, 18 February, 1965

If You've Got Trouble (Ringo)
dropped from soundtrack shortlist
Thursday, 18 February, 1965

You're Going To Lose That Girl (John)
Friday, 19 February, 1965

That Means A Lot (Paul)
dropped from soundtrack shortlist
(+) Saturday, 20 February
Recorded Tuesday, 30 March, 1965
(Later recorded by P.J. Proby)

Help! (John)
Tuesday, 13 April, 1965

I'm Down (Paul)
dropped from actual soundtrack
Monday, 14 June 1965

Wait (John/Paul)
dropped from soundtrack shortlist
Thursday 17 June, 1965

(+) first attempt

BELOW The US soundtrack LP.

In the UK, the soundtrack to *Help!* was released in a single sleeve and without any accompanying liner note. Only on the label did it make any reference to the movie - 'Songs from the film - *Help!*'. Stateside, they went for the whole enchilada. Housed in a thick card gatefold the front cover boldly stated 'Original Motion Picture Soundtrack' as well as listing the song titles 'Help!', 'The Night Before', 'You've Got To Hide Your Love Away', 'I Need You'. 'Another Girl', 'Ticket To Ride, 'You're Gonna Lose That Girl'. There was even room to mention the 'Exclusive Instrumental Music From the Picture's Soundtrack.' Inside the gatefold sleeve, sharing the space with an assortment of film still were two slabs of text.

ON THE LEFT WAS:

'HELP!' Guess where The Beatles are now?

Bermuda!! Austria!! And what are they doing there?

Why are the priests of the terrible Goddess of Kaili interested in The Beatles?

Why is Ringo being pursued to the ends of the earth by a gang of Eastern thugs?

What do they want of him - they aren't fans.

Two leading scientists hope to rule the world.

Paul is threatened by a beetle.

An Eastern beauty saves the boys' lives time and time again.

A channel swimmer ends up in an Alpine lake and Buckingham Palace has a busy day.

When Scotland Yard arrives in the summer Bahamas after unsuccessful manoeuvres on Salisbury Plain they find four Ringos but only one George, one Paul and one John.

When the power crazy scientists arrive in the Alps the boys miraculously escape their deadly weapons.

Will John live to sleep in his pit again?

Will Paul ever get back to his electric organ?

Will George be re-united with his ticker-tape machine?

And Ringo - will he ever play drums again?

(Just in case you haven't seen the movie yet we don't want to spoil the story for you but we will tell you that Ringo is the cause of it all.)

ON THE RIGHT HAND FLAP:-

'HELP!' It's an established fact. Whatever The Beatles do, they do it big, Take their latest film epic, *Help!* With a title like that you'd expect the fun to be fast, frantic and totally unpredictable. It is. What's more, you can be sure that John, Paul, George and Ringo have staged one of the wildest comedy chases ever - from the sunny shores of Nassau to the snowy Alps of Austria and back again.
The plot for the film-making of this full-color saga reads like a success story itself. Men-behind-the-scenes, producer Walter Shenson and director Richard Lester, are the same team who made the fabulous first Beatles film, *A Hard Day's Night*. That film, in The Beatles do-it-big tradition, went on to become as popular with adult audiences as with the younger set and won Academy Award Nominations in two categories.

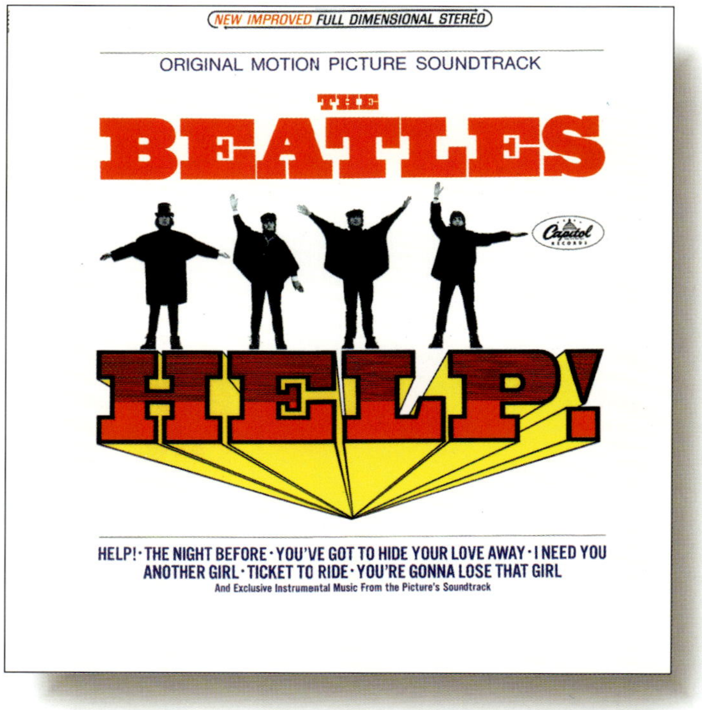

Then, there was the slight predicament over the front cover of the album. The British edition of 'HELP!' has a left-to-right colour photograph of George [H], John [E], Paul [L] and Ringo [P] spelling out the title in semaphores. For the US version, the photograph was much smaller, in monochrome and everyone except George had switched around so that George, Ringo, John and Paul now spelt out HPEL! The Russians went one better. After removing the lads' hats, they reversed the line-up so that Ringo, Paul, John and George were now asking for PLEH!

It doesn't quite end there. A seldom-repeated urban myth suggests that someone employed in EMI Records' art department and, working from modified versions of Robert Freeman's photographs, mocked up at least two alternative album covers. The first had the Fab Four spelling out FUCK!, the second, SHIT! Someone, it is rumoured, almost sent the artwork of one of these covers to the printers, but, hesitated when realising it could be more than just a sackable offense.

In October, it was put up as the official UK entry at the annual Rio de Janeiro Film Festival where it shared the Grand Prix with a French movie. Lester didn't have to share his award as Top Director with anyone else from his profession.

A certified box office success, 'Help!' received favourable reviews. However the use of colour didn't altogether compensate for the freshness of *A Hard Day's Night.* This, in turn, begged the question, whether The Beatles had a long-term future in movies. Precisely, in which direction they would develop was a riddle not even the protagonists themselves could answer!

LEFT John impresses everyone with his new microphone.

ABOVE The Beatles take Eleanor Bron on a Magical Mystery Tour.

HELP!

A United Artists Release
A Walter Shenson-Subafilms Production
Eastmancolour

Director:	Richard Lester
Producer:	Walter Shenson

CAST

John Lennon:	*John*
Paul McCartney:	*Paul*
George Harrison:	*George*
Ringo Starr:	*Ringo*
Leo McKern:	*Clang*
Eleanor Bron:	*Ahme*
Victor Spinetti:	*Foot*
Roy Kinnear:	*Algernon*
Patrick Cargill:	*Superintendent*
John Bluthal:	*Blutha*
Alfie Bass:	*Doorman at Restaurant*
Warren Mitchell:	*Abdul*
Peter Copley:	*Jeweller*
Bruce Lacey:	*Lawn Mover*
Mal Evans:	*Channel Swimmer*

CREDITS

Director	Richard Lester
Production Company	Walter Shenson Films Subafilms
Producer	Walter Shenson
Production Manager	John Pellatt
Assistant Director	Clive Reed
Story	Marc Behm
Scriptwriter	Marc Behm Charles Wood
Photography	David Watkin
Colour Consultant and Titles	Robert Freeman
Editor	John Victor Smith
Art Director	Ray Simm
Songs	John Lennon Paul McCartney
Music Director	Ken Thorne
Music Editor	Barrie Vince
Costumes	Julie Harris Dinah Greet Arthur Newman
Sound	H.L.Bird Stephen Dalby Don Challis Bill Blunden
Length	8280 feet
Time	92 minutes
UK Premiere	29 July, 1965

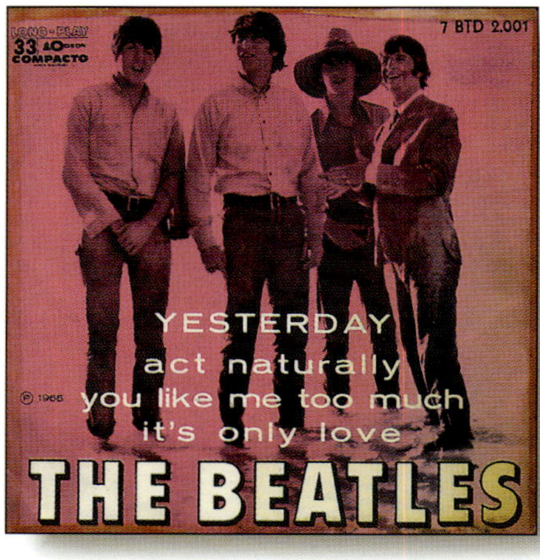

TOP ROW FROM LEFT TO RIGHT Various different versions of the single *'Yesterday'*: French, Spanish and Mexican.

TOP FROM LEFT TO RIGHT Brazilian version of *'Yesterday'*, *'Help!'* EP and French *'Help!'* single.

HELP!

Parlophone PCM 1255 (mono)
PCS 3071 (stereo)
Produced: George Martin
Released: 6 August, 1965

SIDE ONE

1 **Help!** (John)
Tuesday, 13 April, 1965

2 **The Night Before** (Paul)
Wednesday, 17 February, 1965

3 **You've Got To Hide Your Love Away** (John)
Thursday, 18 February, 1965

4 **I Need You** (George)
Monday, 15 February, 1965

5 **Another Girl** (Paul)
Monday, 15 February, 1965

6 **You're Going To Lose That Girl** (John)
Friday, 19 February, 1965

7 **Ticket To Ride** (John)
Monday, 15 February, 1965

SIDE TWO

1 **Act Naturally** (Ringo)
Thursday, 17 June, 1965

2 **It's Only Love** (John)
Tuesday, 15 June, 1965

3 **You Like Me Too Much** (George)
dropped from actual soundtrack
Wednesday, 17 February, 1965

4 **Tell Me What You See** (John/Paul)
dropped from actual soundtrack
Thursday, 18 February, 1965

5 **I've Just Seen A Face** (Paul)
Monday, 14 June, 1965

6 **Yesterday** (Paul)
Monday, 14 June, 1965

7 **Dizzy Miss Lizzy** (John)
Monday, 10 May, 1965

ABOVE FROM LEFT TO RIGHT Various different versions of the 'Help!' LP; German, Swiss and Japanese.

US VERSION

Capitol MAS 2386 (mono)
SMAS 2386 (stereo)

SIDE ONE
1 **Help!**
2 **The Night Before**
3 **From Me To You Fantasy** (instrumental)*
4 **You've Got To Hide Your Love Away**
5 **I Need You**
6 **In The Tyrol** (instrumental)*
introducing Wagner's Overture to Act III of 'Lohengrin' Beatles style

SIDE TWO
1 **Another Girl**
2 **Another Hard Day's Night** (instrumental)*
3 **Ticket To Ride**
4 **The Bitter End/You Can't Do That** (instrumental)*
5 **You're Going To Lose That Girl**
6 **The Chase** (instrumental)*

(*) *The Ken Thorne Orchestra*

UK 45s

A: **Ticket To Ride**
B: **Yes It Is** (John/Paul/George)
dropped from actual soundtrack
Monday, 15 February, 1965
Parlophone R5265
Released: 9 April, 1965

A: **Help!**
B: **I'm Down** (Paul)
dropped from actual soundtrack
Monday, 14 June 1965
Parlophone R5305
Released: 23 July, 1965

US 45s

A: **Ticket To Ride**
B: **Yes It Is**
Capitol 5407
Released: 19 April. 1965

A: **Help!**
B: **I'm Down**
Capitol 5476
Released: 19 July, 1965

A: **Yesterday**
B: **Act Naturally**
Capitol 5498
Released: 13 September, 1965

UK EPs

YESTERDAY
Parlophone GEP 8948
Released: 4 March, 1966
A: **Yesterday**
Act Naturally
B: **You Like Me Too Much**
It's Only Love

Production note
The following material was also recorded during the *'Help!'* soundtrack sessions.

(**) **If You've Got Trouble** (Ringo)
dropped from soundtrack shortlist
Thursday, 18 February, 1965

(**) **That Means A Lot** (Paul)
dropped from soundtrack shortlist
(+) *Saturday, 20 February*
Recorded Tuesday, 30 March, 1965
(Later recorded by P.J. Proby)

Wait (John/Paul)
dropped from soundtrack shortlist
Thursday 17, June, 1965

Bad Boy (John)
Monday, 10 May, 1965

(+) first attempt
(**) still unreleased

7 The Film That Never Was: TWO
A TALENT FOR LOVING

In February 1965, just days before they started work on their still-untitled second full-length movie, it was revealed that The Beatles' third movie would be a grand-slam, all-action western. Scheduled to go into production some time in 1966, an adaptation of Richard Condon's novel *A Talent For Loving*, so the world was informed, was currently in preparation. The scenario of *A Talent For Loving* was based upon a real-life incident and concerned an arduous 1,400-mile overland horse-race that took place in 1871 between the Rio Grande and Mexico City. The affection of a glamourous girl was the victor's spoils, a role yet to be cast. While it still had to be decided which one of the Beatles would carry off such a coveted trophy, it had already been unanimously agreed that the Fab Four wouldn't have to acquire American accents for their new roles. For the sake of authenticity, the characters would be four Liverpudlians who came to the West as pioneers.

Condon, who wrote the critically acclaimed Reds-under-the-beds conspiracy *The Manchurian Candidate* (starring Frank Sinatra and Laurence Harvey), was said to be working away feverishly, in Geneva, on the screenplay of *A Talent For Loving*. The world held a collective breath! *A Talent For Loving*, stressed the official report, would be the first of a number of movies that The Beatles would make exclusively for Pickfair Films - a new movie production company set up by Brian Epstein and (now one-time) United Artists executive Bud Ornstein together with James Isherwood. (Possibly a UA-funded operation as the name Pickfair suggested legendary partners Mary Pickford and Douglas Fairbanks).

ABOVE The Beatles caught horsing around in America.

Aside from returning to Liverpool to shoot the opening sequences, it was said that Ornstein's long-established Spanish connections were already busying themselves scouting for possible locations. Naturally! Most press stories were accompanied by recent photographs of a grinning Ringo wearing a Stetson and brandishing a pair of ornate Colt revolvers. It was emphasised that *A Talent For Loving* would not be the third Beatle vehicle under the terms of their three-picture deal with United Artists. That third (and final) movie for United Artists was scheduled to go before the cameras in Autumn 1965. Its title? As yet, unknown!

As none of The Beatles appeared to be available for comment or supply a printable one liner, in a flippant moment, Richard Condon suggested that, 'the British public should write to their MPs suggesting who should get the girl and have the whole thing settled in Parliament!' Things never got that far down the line. In June 1965, a brief statement was circulated to the media, the contents of which explained that plans to film *A Talent For Loving* in the autumn had been cancelled. The reason? As most of the movie had to be filmed on location in Spain, it was now felt that the weather would not be reliable. But wasn't that the reason Spain was chosen in the first instance? The Beatles, insisted Brian Epstein somewhat vaguely, were working on alternative plans, which would be made public at a later date.

Meanwhile, schedules were being prepared for the 29 July premiere of *Help!* which would be held for the benefit of the Variety Club of Great Britain and the Dockland Settlement Fund.

8

The TV Cartoon Series

SEE YOU LATER, ANIMATOR

On 11 November, 1964, it was reported that US-based King Features Syndicate had secured the television animation rights to The Beatles and was busily preparing a half-hour programme series for night-time network to be aired next season. This projected series of cartoons would follow on from *A Hard Day's Night* with the four lead characters based on the personalities of John, Paul, George and Ringo. The Beatles, said a King Feature representative, would 'perform' a minimum of two songs per episode. Some of them brand new, promised the producers, the remainder being those already dear to the hearts of their countless fans. Working from Peter Sander's original character models, it took 70 artists to interpret the animated on-screen action; each half-hour episode taking one month to create.

With the four individuals meticulously created in such a manner so as not to prove a disappointment to the fans, the plot of most episodes was based around a Beatles' song, a unique selling point but also an in-built restriction on the extent of the precisely timed animated action. Supervising director Jack Stokes, set out the ground rules: **"As far as I'm concerned, the sponsors paid for the Beatle tracks and the kids want to hear them, so anything else must suffer before the music. It would have been marvellous to start with rough stories and then get The Beatles to ad lib dialogue, but the results might have been too offbeat."**

While both *A Hard Day's Night* and *Help!* proved instant box-office smashes Stateside, the fact remained that the majority of young American audiences admitted to being somewhat perplexed by the Fab Four's Liverpudlian patois. King Features neatly sidestepped this problem by hiring American actor Paul Frees to supply the voices of John and George while British character actor and comedian,

Lance Percival took on the guise of Paul and Ringo. Furthermore, the makers resisted the temptation to produce sophisticated, way-out films. One US sponsor painstakingly told Jack Stokes, when he embarked upon the series, that he should never lose sight of the age group these cartoons were directly aimed at. **"Make it 3,000 miles long and 2,000 miles wide - the size of the States,"** was the final word on the subject.

Of the 52 episodes of The Beatles cartoon series, half were made in Britain while the remaining 26 were created by independent teams of Australian and Canadian animators using illustrated character models as production guides. Each comprised between four to seven drawings and was accompanied by a series of comments and guide lines (shown on following pages).

The first series of Beatles cartoons premiered on US TV in September 1965 and shot straight to the front of the ratings where it remained virtually unchallenged, only briefly slipping into second position, during the World Baseball Series.

In later years, after The Beatles split, New York-based John Lennon remarked about how much he genuinely enjoyed parking himself in front of the television and watching the re-runs of this cartoon series.

ABOVE John checks out the story-boards.

OPPOSITE PAGE The real Beatles are the ones with the drinks in their hands.

JOHN

- John, especially when delivering important lines, really looks the leader. Feet apart, hands on hips, chin up, looking down his nose. With a slightly mocking expression. (This pose can also be used when he is pointing.)

- Notice distance between John's mouth and nose.

- When facing front he uses a sly, sideways look to talk to somebody.

- Pulls funny faces especially after giving orders, which he immediately wipes off. He also looks the other way before giving an order.

- Slightly queer 'showbiz' gestures can be used in long shot. Mostly with hands. Gives feeling that John doesn't take his job as leader seriously.

- John moves with fast, jerky, almost aggressive movements.

- John never sits - he slouches.

PAUL

- Paul is the most poised and stylish Beatle. When he talks he uses his hands, with fingers spread to express what he is saying. He always looks straight at whoever he is talking to. He is the one who gets excited when John suggests anything.

- He doesn't really walk - he skips.

- Paul is the same height as George.

- When Paul is in the background he stands with feet together and arms folded.

- Paul sits as though he is ready to jump up and get on with whatever is happening.

- When he is making his own suggestions and comments, especially ones suggesting mischief, he covers up by assuming a mock innocent look, eyes wide and head tilted to one side.

- He tends to put his hand to his mouth when he is excited.

GEORGE

- Head always tilted forward.
- George never looks at who he is talking to. But his shoulders, which are hunched when he is in a standing or leaning pose, can indicate the direction.
- George is the same height as Paul.
- George is very loose limbed and angular when he walks. Remember his legs are long and thin. An emphasis on the knees will help the angular appearance.
- He often closes his eyes for short periods when he is talking.
- George nearly always gives the impression of frowning. This is because his eyebrows thicken as they reach his nose. Notice the way the eyes are drawn.
- Notice distance between nose and mouth. His mouth is always lop-sided.
- George never stands. He is always leaning against something. Shoulders hunched, hands in pockets. Legs crossed.
- Even when George sits, he looks awkward and angular.

RINGO

- Ringo is the nice gentle Beatle, although he always looks rather sad.
- Ringo always looks a bit disjointed whether walking or standing.
- Ringo walks in a Groucho Marx pose.
- Keep upper lip protruding. Keep Ringo's neck thin to help the disjointed look. Keep hair at back long and shaggy.
- When Ringo laughs, having made a funny remark, he squints his eyes.
- When Ringo stands he always droops forward. His clothes tend to look as though they are a bit too big.
- Normally, Ringo is always deadpan but should an expression be required the main movement is arching the eyebrows. Keep the mouth in a wavy line.
- Ringo sits normally, slightly hunched.
- Ringo is a head smaller than George and Paul.

9 The Film That Never Was: THREE SHADES OF A PERSONALITY

During the first week of April, Walter Shenson made it very clear that there would be no new Beatle movie in 1966. With a suitable property still to be agreed upon, production had been put back until some time in October, meaning that a new film wouldn't hit the screens until mid-1967. *A Talent For Loving* was definitely yesterday's news. Walter Shenson justified his decision as producer thus: **"I have had several more meetings with the boys and we have gone over a number of fresh suggestions for stories but everything has been rejected. At the moment we have absolutely nothing suitable. Brian Epstein says we should go ahead after The Beatles return from their American tour at the beginning of September but they will need time to write some songs and record before shooting can begin, so it looks like an October start - and that, of course, depends upon us finding the right story. We have turned down everything from 'The Beatles In The Army' to 'The Beatles Meet Elvis Presley'."**

In the first week of May, Shenson made public the problems of locating that elusive script for the Beatles proposed third movie. Whereas, the first two Beatles' movies had been of the visual knockabout variety, for this third time before the cameras, both standards and budgets would be greatly increased.

Walter Shenson

'It's not enough to make a frivolous film or trade on the success of The Beatles generally. We don't have to make a film at this moment and we are all agreed that it's better to make no film at all than make a bad one. We have to be very careful. The Beatles have always been first at everything they've done and they never do what's expected of them. Hollywood is now copying *A Hard Day's Night* while *Help!* was a beautifully visual pop art film, so we want this next film to be just as unexpected as well.'

HAVE THE BEATLES GONE TOO FAR?

From HENRY THODY *NEW YORK, Saturday.*

HAVE the Beatles gone too far this time? America believes they have. When the Beatles arrive in Chicago next Thursday for their third American tour they will undoubtedly be greeted with pickets carrying signs "Down with the Beatles" and "Go home, Beatles."

But, of course, they will also be greeted by the usual screaming, shrilling teenage fans.

Trying to buy a ticket for their Chicago concert was like trying to get a ticket for Wembley last Saturday.

I spoke to Brian Epstein, the Beatles' slim, sun-tanned young manager, today in New York. He had got up from a sick-bed and flown across the Atlantic when he heard of the furore following John Lennon's "We're more popular than Jesus" interview.

Regretted

As a result scores of American disc jockeys in the Deep South "Bible Belt" have banned the Beatles' records. Others are threatening to hold public bonfires to burn their library of Beatle records.

To me, millionaire Mr. Epstein looked like the original man-crying-on-his-way-to-the-bank.

He confessed that the sale of tickets in Memphis, in the *real* deep South, had soared since the religious uproar.

At the same time he regretted that American church-goers had been offended by Lennon's remarks, reprinted in an American teenage magazine this week from a London newspaper interview in March.

Lennon is reported to have said:

"Christianity will go. It will vanish and shrink. I needn't argue about that: I'm right, and I will be proved right. We're more popular than Jesus now—I don't know which will go first Rock 'n Roll or Christianity. Jesus was all right, but his disciples were thick and ordinary."

Brian Epstein explained over nation-wide television that Lennon was really expressing his astonishment that in the last 50 years the Church of England had suffered such a lack of interest, especially among teenagers.

He appeared puzzled how the rumpus all began and said he was concerned over the safety of the Liverpool foursome in the current wild "climate of violence" mood of America.

I spoke to the man who started the anti-Beatles row — Tommy Charles, disc jockey of Station WAQY in the racial trouble spot of Birmingham, Alabama. Mr. Charles, aged 36 ("but I think like a teenager") was the first man to be outraged by Lennon's remark, the first to ban Beatle records, and the first to threaten a public burning of Beatle discs.

Now he has calmed down a bit. "There won't be any public burnings here," he said. "I've had second thoughts. I don't want to be linked with Ku-Klux-Klanism, Nazism or intolerance. I'm not out to hurt John Lennon but his remarks about Jesus stink. You can't make a comparison between Christianity and the top ten."

'Squares'

As I left Manhattan's swank Americana hotel on Seventh Avenue, after talking to Mr. Epstein, I was stopped by a group of Beatle fans waiting outside the hotel. I asked a podgy 16-year-old from Brooklyn, who preferred just to be known as Nancy, what she thought.

"Who goes to church anymore except squares? But everyone goes to see the Beatles," she said.

Her classmate, Barbara Graziano, said: "I'm a Catholic. I go to Mass every Sunday. But for me John Lennon can do no wrong."

John Lennon may not have done religion, nor Britain much good with his hardly diplomatic quotes. But one thing seems certain. In their third barnstorming of the U.S.A. they will again bring back loads and loads of lolly. Perhaps more than ever this time.

Indeed, any new film would have to be infinitely superior to their first two screen adventures. If not, it would have serious repercussions.

Walter Shenson

'The succeeding films will be affected if it's a bad film. And the boys themselves don't want to do anything bad. There will be such a gap between *Help!* and this one that it will have to be good. Also, as the boys say, if they make a bad record, they can always throw the tapes away. But if half-a-million is spent on a film, good or bad it has to go on release.'

Contrary to policy, Shenson indicated that it had now been mutually agreed that in their third film John, Paul, George and Ringo would revert from playing themselves and take on fictitious roles. According to Shenson, the reason that most scripts submitted to him for consideration were promptly rejected was due to the fact that they closely shadowed *A Hard Day's Night* and *Help!* and had the Fab Four close to parodying their familiar selves.

Walter Shenson

'To find a good enough story-line, which has four leading characters, is very difficult. The fault with the scripts that have been submitted hasn't been bad writing, but ignorance of what we are looking for. We are more

ABOVE LEFT Once Public Enemy No. 1 himself - Elvis would later suggest to the FBI that The Beatles were a bad influence on American youth.

less agreed this time that The Beatles should not play The Beatles. They will play four characters who look, think and talk like The Beatles but are different characters. The only other criteria would be that any new Beatles movie would have to be contemporary. They don't want to do a period story. But, the script must be a strong story-line and very different from their first two films. This time, they may not be playing a group.'

On the question of who rejects the material submitted.

'I turn down the obvious ones. Those with some worth are put up to Brian and the boys. So far, I've never been disappointed by them not liking a script. They know what they want - they are, after all, the best judges of themselves - and there's been no script that I've wanted them to do that they've turned down.'

Aware of the rapid decline in the quality of Elvis's conveyor-belt movies, Shenson said:

It would be easy for us to do the same as Elvis does - Elvis in the Army and that sort of thing. Even when he uses a different name in the film, it's basically the same Elvis character. The same with Cliff Richard - on holiday, etc. That wouldn't work with The Beatles. They know it."

ABOVE John's "we're more popular than Jesus" remark provided much ammunition for tabloid cartoonists.

The search for a suitable script continued. Meanwhile, on Thursday, 11 August - the eve of what was to be their last-ever tour - John Lennon used a Chicago press conference to apologise for his previous (inflammatory) 'more popular than Jesus' statement. Tommy Charles, the self-promoting Alabama disc-jockey who first instigated the anti-Beatles/burn-their-records campaign in the wake of Lennon's original remarks, reacted to John's apology as if he was accepting it on behalf of the injured party. Outside the press conference, pro-Beatle fans demonstrated noisily against John's public climb down.

Throughout the summer months, stories circulated that Shenson's search was over and that a script was under consideration, while January 1967 had been provisionally pencilled-in as a possible starting date. The writer of this yet-to-be-titled script - simply referred to as 'Beatles 3' - was Owen Holder, who had previously supplied the screenplay for Richard Lester's *A Funny Thing Happened On The Way To The Forum.* A director had still to be commissioned. One thing was certain, The Beatles would compose the entire musical soundtrack, comprising up to nine new songs plus the incidental background score.

By late October, details of the actual plot began to emerge. One of The Beatles (rumours first suggested Ringo) would play the part of a man who, aside from his real self, suffered a three-way split personality that in turn manifested itself as three very different sides to his character. Those three different 'personalities' would be the other three Beatles. Accordingly, Owen Holder had written four separate story-lines around this workable basic idea, each reflecting The Beatles' individual personalities. The leading lady and various other supporting players were still to be shortlisted. If, as suggested, the Beatles went before the cameras in January 1967, then it was most unlikely that Richard Lester would be available due to previous commitments.

By November, Walter Shenson admitted that neither he or The Beatles had approved the first draft of the script so that the possibility of a finished shooting script was still in the future. Realistically, a January start-up date looked remote, though February was a possibility.

BELOW John guards against making any more controversial statements.

OPPOSITE PAGE The Beatles with yet another image make-over. This time for the suitably psychedelic *'Strawberry Fields Forever'* shoot.

Walter Shensan

'We are still not in any hurry to make this picture. It would be silly, having waited a year for the right idea, to rush ahead to meet some previously announced schedule. Neither The Beatles nor I are in a hurry. When we do it, it will be right.'

Then, quite suddenly, in June 1967, the script had a title and the film had a director. *Shades Of A Personality* was the working title of Owen Holder's original idea. However, contrary to rumour, it wasn't Ringo who was to be cast in the main role but John Lennon, with the other three Beatles portraying his other personalities. As for the director, awarding winning *Blow-Up* moviemaker Michelangelo Antonioni was in the frame and Malaga, Spain was the proposed location. Production would take six months. But with *Magical Mystery Tour* still to be completed and *Yellow Submarine* still to be made, the timing for this project was never right and *Shades Of A Personality* was eventually dropped from The Beatles' things-to-do check list. As Ringo explained at the time: **"The ideas we considered for a film western (*A Talent For Loving*) and for us to play the split personality of one person were fine in theory. But they just didn't work out as a 90-minutes script."**

Against a background of yet another round of tiresome 'Beatles To Split/Beatles Deny Split' rumours, a new player entered the game: Hollywood movie producer Allen Klein. A verbal statement from Klein's lawyer, Marty Machat revealed: **"Mr Klein wants The Beatles. He thinks they can all be film stars, but at the moment it is in the melting pot. Mr Klein, does not want anything to strain the relationship between Mr Epstein or The Beatles. That is the main problem at the moment. That is why he cannot say anything."**

Here was the giveaway. Machat continued. **"I assume The Beatles are under a five-year contract which began in 1962 or 1963. That leaves one year or a year and a half to run."** Machat then went on to outline Klein's future Beatles business plan as if it were already a fait accompli. **"The four Beatles together are much stronger than as individuals. Mr Klein thinks they could be the natural replacements to the Marx Brothers. There has been nothing like them for 15 years."** As to whether or not Klein would be holding talks with Epstein and the Beatles, Machat's guarded reply was, **"I cannot comment on how it will be done."**

Epstein's office fobbed off the story by insisting that the story was all too ridiculous to comment on. Those in the music industry who knew of Klein by reputation viewed the incident as nothing more than the kind of proposed hostile takeover bid more common to city business trading. This would not be the last time the world heard the name Allen Klein.

10

HOW I WON THE WAR

'*How I Won The War* is a tragedy told in comedic terms and a film which most certainly didn't help my career. But, I'm glad I made it.'
Richard Lester

The Beatles gave what was to be their final live concert before an audience of 25,000 fans at San Francisco's Candlestick Park on Monday, 29 August 1966, and immediately jetted back to Britain. True to his claim **'Well, that's it, I'm not a Beatle any more'**, John Lennon flew out to Germany on Monday, 5 September, got his hair cropped the next day and began filming his role as Private Gripweed (opposite Michael Crawford) in *How I Won The War* which Richard Lester both produced and directed.

Made on a budget £400,000, the screenplay was based on a novel by Patrick Ryan which Lester apparently disliked, but retained the name of the characters and a few ideas as the basic plot underwent seven rewrites before he felt he had got a working script. Unfortunately, the movie's vehemently anti-war stance was totally misconstrued by almost everyone and backfired on both Lester and Lennon. Reaching for his book of clichés, one critic regurgitated that tired old chestnut of viewing John Lennon as nothing more substantial than a clown playing Hamlet, while ex-servicemen organisations throughout Britain branded the movie an insult to the war dead - particularly for its use of genuine combat footage of Arnhem, Alamein and Dunkirk.

How I Won The War opened in London's West End to objections raised in Parliament, a National Front stink-bomb being thrown during the screening, followed by the film subsequently being banned by the distributor! Cinema managers refused to show *How I Won The War* on Armistice Day claiming it to be obscene because it was an anti-war film, yet at the same time it was possible to see *The Dirty Dozen,* a film that glorifies the worst elements of war. It was an attitude that Lester still describes as 'cynical and sick.' However, he can see why so many people voiced their objections: **"If half the people who complained had actually gone to see it, I'd have had a smash hit..."** And, he was probably right. *How I Won The War* wasn't the first (or the last) film to be condemned by those who hadn't paid the price of admission. And it's usually these protesters who campaign the loudest.

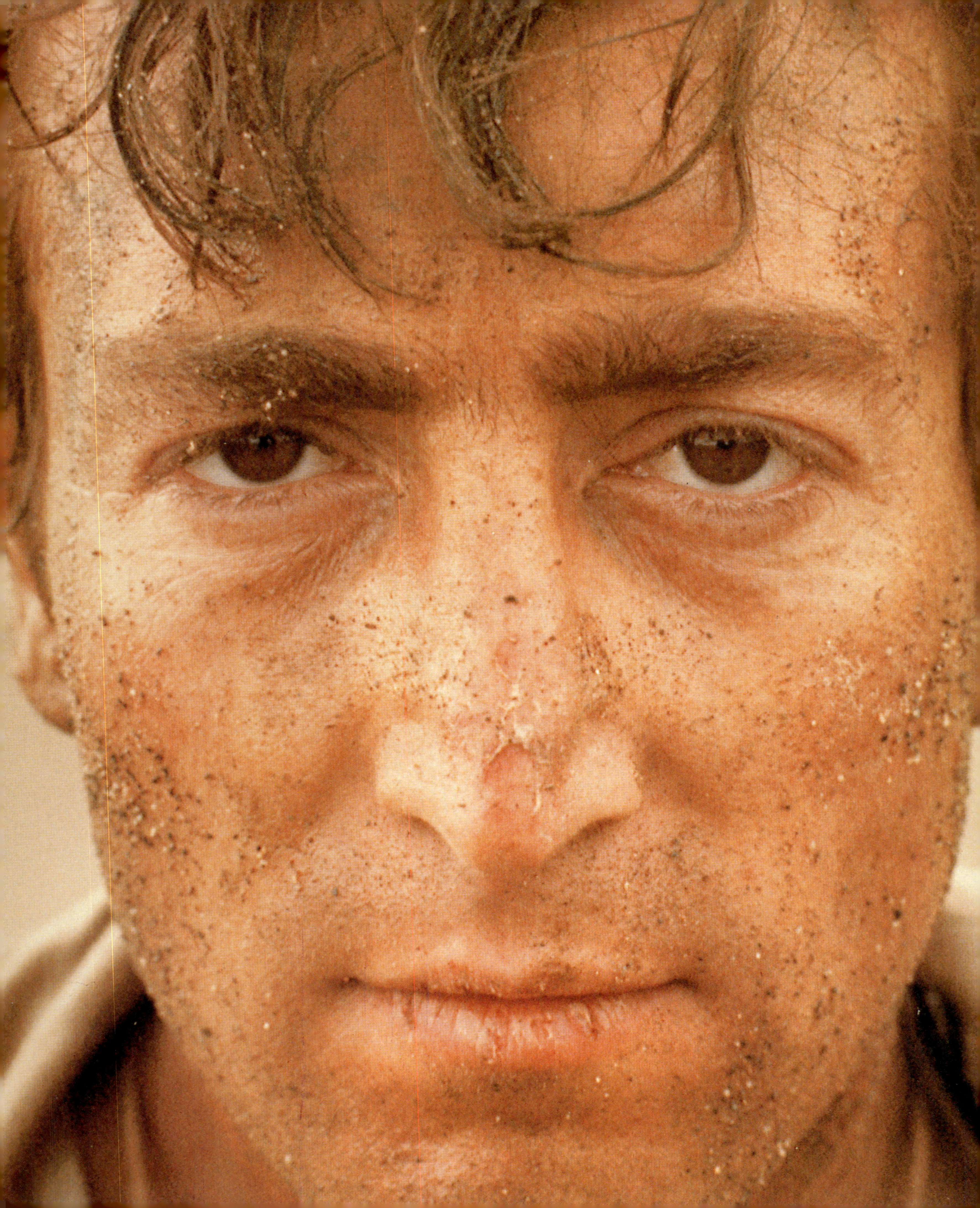

Richard Lester

'I think people have forgotten, but in the middle sixties - it was the 20th anniversary of the end of World War II and there were an awful lot of BBC documentaries taking Monty back to El Alamein and letting him walk along the sands in his suit, talking about how he won the war. And, it was this obscenity of nostalgia that my film was attacking. All that jingoism and the marketing of war as a piece of nostalgic exercise. It was all pretty near the knuckle. That's what *How I Won The War* was all about and John agreed with that.'

Under Lester's direction, it was a film which used the technique of Brechtian alienation and worked so well that, almost instantly, it succeeded in alienating its intended audience.

'One thing I was sure of, I didn't want it to be a film where - like most war films - a band of disparate people come together and then get forged in the crucible of danger to become best pals. That's why, in the middle of these important scenes, every actor turns to the audience and says, "you knew this was going to happen, didn't you?" so as to stop that romanticism. It was the most unromantic film I could possibly make and I'm still very proud of it.'

At the time of it's release, Richard Lester told *The Sunday Times*:

'We have made a genuinely pacifist film. Everyone involved came to feel they were on a crusade. I didn't want to do a tank opera, I wanted to show war without kicks. If I fell under a bus tomorrow this is what I'd want to be judged by. I wanted to show that there was another side of the coin, that war is not a cosy romp as so many films seem to depict it. I feel very strongly about it myself. But when I was making it I didn't think about the possible effect on people who tend to glamourise their memories of the war days. I just went ahead and did it. We always remember the things we want to. I hope to show people some of the things they may not choose to remember and get things into perspective again.'

Out of a network of 260 cinemas, Lester estimates that less than 100 screened *How I Won The War.* Had he been able to remake it, he insisted he wouldn't have changed the tone and that its black-comedy stance was correct. However, the day after its West End premiere, he confessed:

'I'm sorry in one way that John Lennon was in the film because it creates an imbalance. The part just seemed to fit John, though I didn't want to make a film with a Beatle in it.'

ABOVE With his familiar mop-top cropped, John takes on the guise of Private Gripweed.

ABOVE Roy Kinnear and John Lennon celebrate the Glorious Twelfth and a pheasant shoot.

Richard Lester

'At one point, while we were making the movie, I turned to John and said, 'if you really wanted to you could either be a good serious or comic actor,' and his reply was, 'I know I probably could, but, what a silly thing to do!'

'And, we were only into the first week of shooting, and I thought to myself, 'God, if he thinks it's silly, then how on earth am I going to get through the schedule!'

Lennon agreed to the project in the first instance because he feared that following the Beatles' last-ever tour, he might find himself at a loose end and making a movie with Lester would help keep him occupied. Amongst other things, Lennon bided his time by writing 'Strawberry Fields Forever' during breaks in the filming.

ABOVE A series of Italian billboard posters for *'How I Won The War' ('Come Ho Vinto La Guerra').*

* * * * *

How I Won The War **was the very first of three films that Richard Lester produced himself. The other two were *Petulia* (1968) and *The Bed Sitting Room* (1969). *Petulia* which starred Julie Christie was the American entry for the Cannes Film Festival on the day of the May Riots at which point the festival collapsed in turmoil. Originally, Lester's third independent production was going to Joe Orton's *Up Against It* (more later) and when that didn't work out as planned, he turned to Spike Milligan's controversial play and filmed that instead.**

Richard Lester

'*The Bed Sitting Room* was something that everybody hated, but then suddenly in the Eighties it was voted by three out of a panel of 50 critics as one of the best 10 films ever made! And, I thought, where were you when it first came out?'

'Same with *Petulia* which was voted the third best film of the Sixties/Seventies right behind *The Godfather* and *The Graduate* and yet it didn't do that well the first time round!'

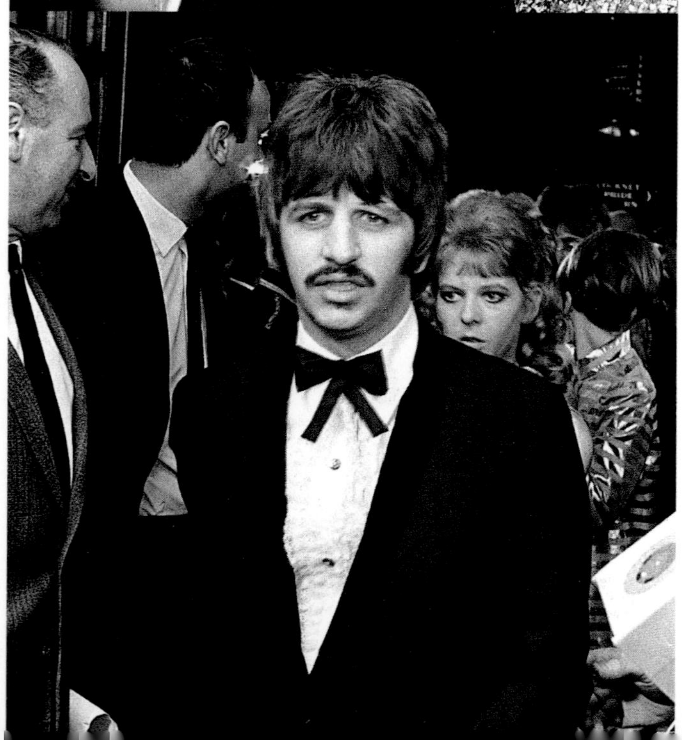

HOW I WON THE WAR

Petersham Films

Director/Producer: Richard Lester

CAST

Michael Crawford	*Lt. Ernest Goodbody*
John Lennon	*Private Gripweed*
Roy Kinnear	*Clapper*
Lee Montague	*Transom*
Jack MacGowran	*Juniper*
Michael Horden	*Grapple*
Jack Hedley	*Melancholy Musketeer*
Karl-Michael Vogler	*Odlebog*
Ronald Lacey	*Spool*
James Cossins	*Drogue*
Ewan Hooper	*Dooley*
Alexander Knox	*American General*
Robert Hardy	*British General*
Sheila Hancock	*Mrs. Clapper's Friend*
Charles Dyer	*Flappy-Trousered Man*
William Dysart	*Paratrooper*
Paul Daneman	*Skipper*
Peter Craven	*Staff Officer*
Jack May	*Toby*
Richard Pearson	*Old Man at Alamein*
Pauline Taylor	*Woman in Desert*
John Ronane	*Operator*
Norman Chappell	*Soldier at Alamein*
Bryan Pringle	*Reporter*
Fanny Carby	*Mrs. Clapper*
Dandy Nichols	*1st Old Lady*
Gretchen Franklin	*2nd Old Lady*
John Junkin	*Large Child*
John Trenaman	*Driver*
Mick Dillon	*1st Replacement*
Kenneth Colley	*2nd Replacement*

CREDITS

Director	Richard Lester
Production Company	Petersham Films
Producer	Richard Lester
Associate Producer	Denis O'Dell
Production Managers	Hubert Froelich
	Roberto Roberts
Assistant Director	Jose Lopez Rodero
Scriptwriter	Charles Wood
Original Novel	Patrick Ryan
Cinematography	David Watkins
Editor	John Victor Smith
Art Directors	Philip Harrison
	John Stoll
Special Effects	Eddie Fowlie
Music	Ken Thorne
Sound Recording	Les Hammond
Length	9941 feet
Running Time	110 minutes

11

THE FAMILY WAY

Paul McCartney composed the basic themes for this movie, giving them over to George Martin to write the orchestral scores and supply further incidental music. As the plot was set in the North of England, it was McCartney's suggestion that the treatment should have a brass band sound. However, there was a shortfall in the material that McCartney handed Martin. Almost immediately, Martin told McCartney that what was required was 'a wistful little tune' and, that unless he came up with something sharpish, he (Martin) would write one of his very own. That sparked McCartney into overdrive who quickly furnished Martin with 'a sweet little fragment of a waltz tune' and the score was completed.

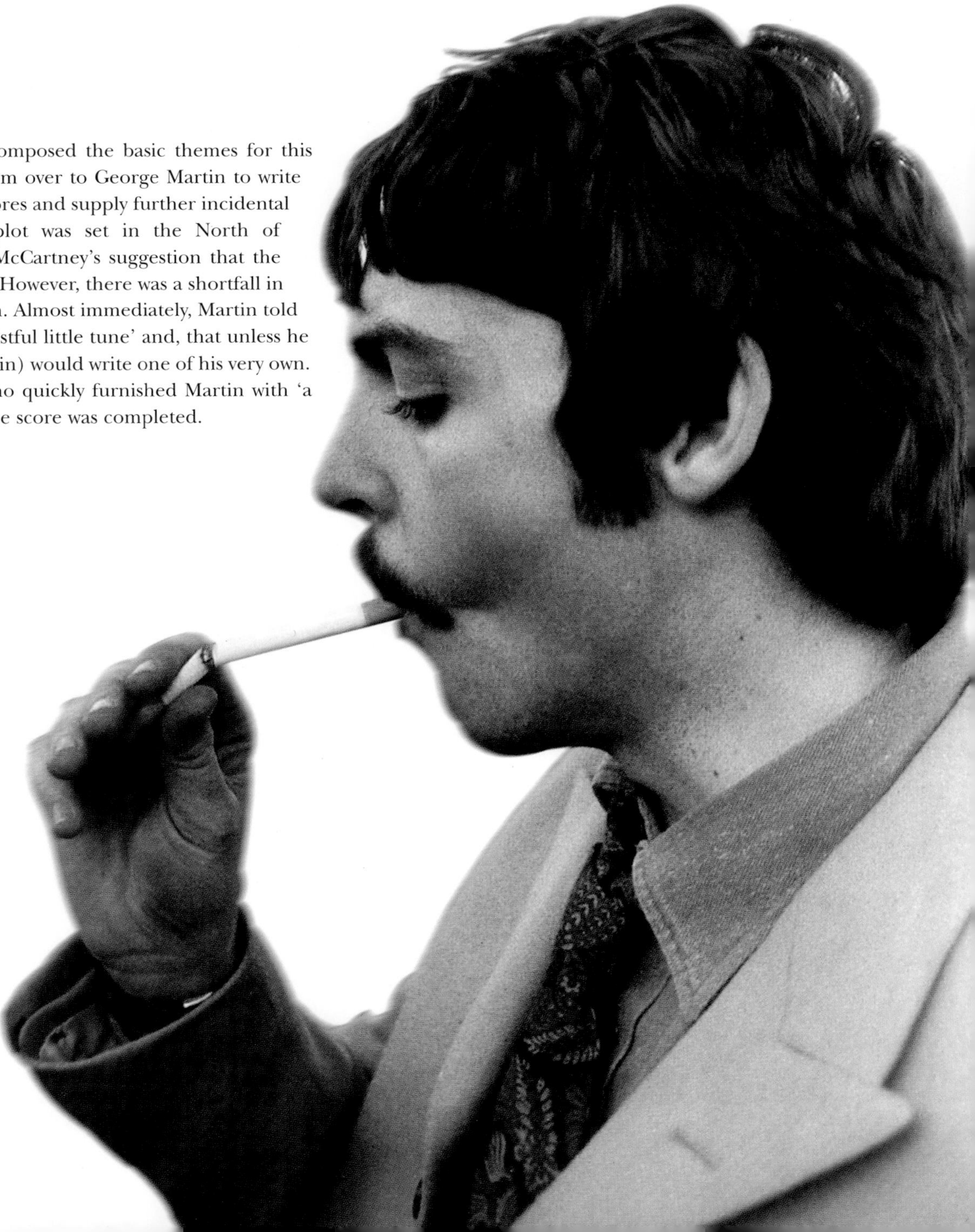

ABOVE The soundtrack LP.

OPPOSITE PAGE Hywel and Hayley in ecstatic mood.

THE FAMILY WAY

Jambox Films

Director	Roy Boulting
Producer	John Boulting

CAST

Hywel Bennett	*Arthur Fitton*
Hayley Mills	*Jenny Piper*
John Mills	*Ezra Fitton*
Marjorie Rhodes	*Lucy Fitton*
Murray Head	*Geoffrey Fitton*
Avril Angers	*Liz Piper*
John Comer	*Leslie Piper*
Wilfred Pickles	*Uncle Fred*
Barry Foster	*Joe Thompson*
Liz Fraser	*Molly Thompson*
Colin Gordon	*Mr. Hutton*
Robin Parkinson	*Mr. Phillips*
Andy Bradford	*Eddie*
Lesley Daine	*Dora*
Ruth Trouncer	*Marriage Guidance Councellor*
Harry Locke	*Mr. Stubbs*
Maureen O'Reilly	*Miss Hunt*
Michael Cadman	*Len*
Thorley Walters	*The Vicar*
Hazel Bainbridge	*Mrs. Bell*
Ruth Gower	*Mrs. Pike*
Diana Coupland	*Mrs. Rose*
Helen Booth	*Mrs. Lee*
Margaret Lacey	*Mrs. Harris*

CREDITS

Director	Roy Boulting
Production Company	Jambox
Producer	John Boulting
Assistant Director	Peter Price
Adapter	Roy Boulting Jefferey Dell
Screenplay & Original Play	Bill Naughton
Cinematography	Harry Waxman
Editor	Ernest Hosler
Art Director	Alan Withy
Music	Paul McCartney
Music Director	George Martin
Sound	Christopher Lancaster
Sound Recording	David Bowen John Aldred
Length	10260 feet (3127 metres)

12

CANDY

After his success in *A Hard Day's Night,* there was never any real doubt that Ringo, more than any other Beatle, possessed a natural comedic flair. The deep nasal drone of his voice was just as expressive as his mournful, hang-dog face. However, he could crack a smile that instantly illuminated a scene. While genuinely at ease in front of a camera, precisely how to showcase Ringo's acting abilities proved the major problem. Unfortunately, there didn't appear to be anyone on hand with the same perceptive grasp as Richard Lester.

Ringo didn't so much as "go Hollywood", but was unwittingly seduced by the promise of hanging out with a pack of celebrities as well known to the public as himself. It's not everyday that a drummer - and occasional singer - is cast in the same movie as Marlon Brando and Richard Burton. The cast of *Candy* may have been seen to be stellar, but, sadly the script was not. Buck Henry's screen play of Terry Southern's hot novel should have proved a fail-safe formula, but was found to be wanting.

This was a period when star-spotting movies were supposed to be hip (or at least were thought to be by those accepting mis-cast cameos), but in fact such vehicles became an embarrassment to most everyone involved .

John had made *How I Won The War* while Paul and George had dabbled in composing soundtracks (*The Family Way* and *Wonderwall* respectively), so Ringo grabbed at the opportunity to play Emmanuel, the Mexican gardener in *Candy.*

To his credit, Ringo did what was expected of him, while Brando was cast as an Indian guru (Grindl) and Burton as Old Nick (McPhisto). Other all-star lurkers included James Coburn, Walter Matthau, Charles Aznavour, John Houston, Elsa Martinelli and Anita Pallenberg. The common denominator was Candy (Ewa Aulin) - a blonde haired/doe-eyed, sexually accommodating ingenue who willingly shared her favour with most of the cast at the drop of her clothes. One scene which involved Ringo attempting to 'entertain' Candy on a pool table brought a whole new perspective to the art of miscuing.

ABOVE The soundtrack LP.

OPPOSITE PAGE Ringo getting into character as Emmanuel the Mexican gardener.

C-31

CANDY

Selmur Pictures
Dear Film
Films Corona
Technicolor

Director	Christian Marquand
Producer	Robert Haggiag

CAST

Ewa Aulin	*Candy*
Marlon Brando	*Grindl*
Richard Burton	*McPhisto*
James Coburn	*Dr. Krankeit*
Walter Matthau	*General Smight*
Charles Aznavour	*The Hunchback*
John Houston	*Dr. Dunlap*
John Austin	Daddy/Uncle Jack
Elsa Martinelli	*Livia*
Ringo Starr	*Emmanuel*
Enrico Maria Salerno	*Jonathan J. John*
Sugar Ray Robinson	*Zero*
Anita Pallenberg	*Nurse Bullock*
Lea Padovani	*Silvia*
Florinda Bolkan	*Lolita*
Maril Toto	*Conchita*
Nicoletta Machiavelli	*Marquita*
Umberto Orsini	*1st Hood*
Joey Forman	*The Cop*
Fabian Dean	*The Sergeant*
Neal Noorlac	*Harold*
Peter Dane	*Luther*
Peggy Nathan	*Miss Quimby*
Tony Foutz	*1st Weirdo*
Tom Keyes	*2nd Weirdo*
Micaela Pignatelli	*Girl*
Mark Salvage	*Dr. Harris*
Enzo Fiermonte	*2nd Hood*
Living Theatre	

BELOW Ringo (Emmanuel) and Ewa Aulin(Candy) in less-than-romantic encounter.

OPPOSITE PAGE Grindl (Marlon Brando) manages to levitate Candy (Ewa Aulin).

13

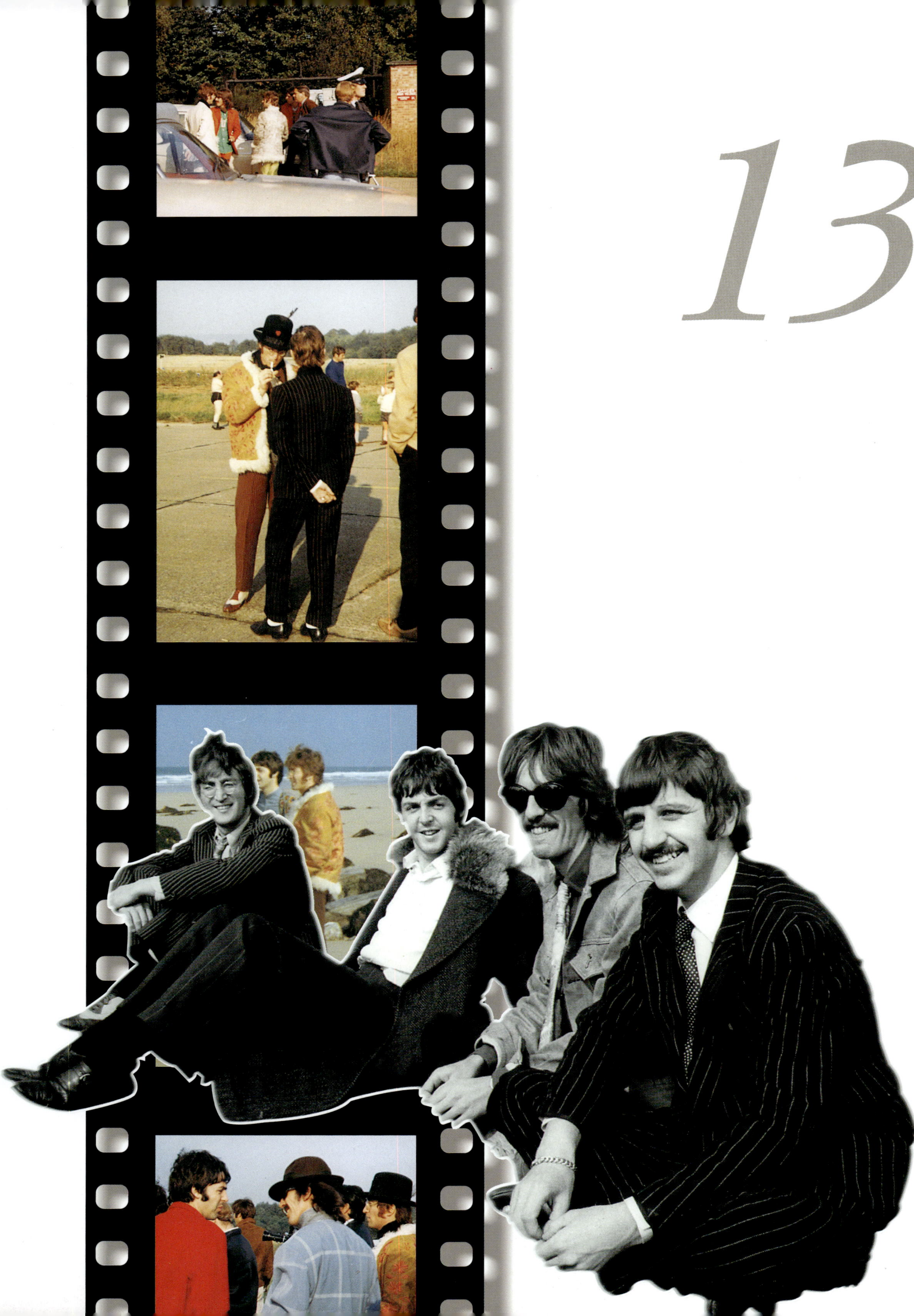

MAGICAL MYSTERY TOUR

'If The Beatles' professional career were to be plotted on a graph, *Magical Mystery Tour* was definitely a dip.'
George Martin

Brian Epstein had become increasingly depressed following The Beatles' decision to stop touring following a string of US stadium dates in August 1966 which culminated at San Francisco's Candlestick Park on Monday, the 29th. George Martin may well have been the one who was in control in the studio, while Richard Lester defined how the public believed the Fab Four to be in real life. As for Epstein, his forte was out there on the road fronting the entire operation like some heroic and chivalrous English general. Epstein's public image couldn't have been further removed from reality.

In private, Epstein's increased drug indulgence and rampant promiscuity had by now greatly heightened his paranoia. Then there was the vexed question of the Guru. With the giggling Maharishi Mehesh Yogi having latched onto the Beatles' bandwagon, Epstein felt that he was rapidly losing his grip on the situation and that he would have no alternative but to reinvent his role on a grand and artistic scale. Movies seemed the obvious route. With Allen Klein still lurking in the background playing devil's advocate, Epstein was also plagued by unconfirmed rumours that The Beatles would automatically seek a new manager when their original five-year contract with him came up for renewal on 8 October, 1967.

Unbeknown to Epstein, the most audacious of these stories were being wilfully circulated by those spurned acquaintances and business rivals who delighted in winding him up and then observing the anticipated results. Despite his fears, Epstein knew that though the Beatles desired more freedom, more independence (which would later be partly realised with the inauguration of their own Apple Corp), they weren't about to desert him publicly. It was just that he was becoming increasingly aware that he was no longer central to their many requirements. Each had their own court.

BELOW Paul anticipates '70's disco craze for knitted Tank Tops.

TOP The Beatles and the Magical Mystery Tourists.

ABOVE The soundtrack LP.

Richard Lester

'Right from the beginning, I'm not sure how many decisions Brian Epstein ever made. John was a very strong personality and the boys themselves, as a four-headed group of people, did very much have a say as to what they wanted to do. It would have been very hard to shove an idea down those four throats. Initially, there was a sense that Brian Epstein was this extraordinary businessman with a clear view of how to mould and shape this phenomenon. But, from my experience, I would think that Brian didn't dictate anything to the boys.'

The Beatles were spending the week-end in Bangor, North Wales studying Transcendental Meditation under the guidance of the Maharishi when Epstein died unexpectedly on Sunday, 27 August, 1967. *Magical Mystery Tour* was to be part of the immediate fall out. To coin a cliché - it really was a case of the show must go on and when, just four days after their manager's death, The Beatles met to discuss their immediate plans. Right away, it was agreed to continue with the *Magical Mystery Tour* which had been put on hold when the four of them had decided to pottle off to India in February. As it transpired, it proved a most shambolic adventure.

Long-time confidant and now Apple supremo, Neil Aspinall put things into perspective when he stated: **"We went out to make a film and nobody had the vaguest idea of what it was all about. What we should have been filming, if anything, was all the confusion, because that was the REAL mystery tour."** This was Aspinall's reference to Lennon ripping the signs off the coach in an effort to thwart the convoy of reporters that tailgated the tour and the traffic chaos that ensued whenever they stopped to film, eat or take a leak. It quickly became apparent that with Epstein gone, there was no day-to-day internal organisation.

McCartney, who had become intrigued by the San Francisco-based Merry Pranksters (LSD chomping New Age travellers), knocked up the bare bones of what was to become the *Magical Mystery Tour*, on a return flight from the States to Britain.

Richard Lester

'Denis O'Dell was the Associate Producer of *How I Won The War* and when I went off to do *Petulia* with Julie Christie, he was asked to take over and become the head of films at Apple and that's when they decided they would do *Magical Mystery Tour.* And I would hear Denis on the phone to Paul or whoever, saying "I've found a great place...we're going to film it all in an old off-shore military fortification tower"...then it would be "were going to Egypt to shoot it in the giant Pyramids, but I've only got eight days to get all these crews together"...then the next day they would change their minds - he went crazy. From the moment that they finally decided to make it till the time the first shots were made was only two weeks. It went off totally unprepared and half-cocked.'

TOP ROW George and John model the very latest in trendy clothes and head gear.

ABOVE *'Magical Mystery Tour'* EP featuring *'I Am The Walrus'* and booklet.

The way Lennon saw *Magical Mystery Tour* evolve was that McCartney and Mal Evans worked out the basic ideas between them, before presenting them to John, George and Ringo

John Lennon

'Paul had a tendency to come along and say, he'd written ten songs, let's record now. And, I'd said, "well, give us a few days to knock a few off" or something like that.'

'Paul would say, "Well, here's the segment, you write a little piece for that. "And I thought, "fuckin' Ada, I've never made a film, what's he mean?"'

So Lennon went off and wrote the dream sequence for the fat lady and all the things with the spaghetti.

The Tour began on Monday, 11 September when the cast and crew hopped on board a coach in Central London and headed West steering a course through Hampshire, Devon, Cornwall and Somerset. They filmed almost immediately on an ad hoc basis over the next five days with villages and towns such as Widcombe on Dartmoor, Bodmin, Newquay, Watergate Bay, Porth and Taunton among the favoured locations. Additional filming took place later in the month at Paul Raymond's Revuebar in London's Soho (Jan

ABOVE Local fans go to extreme lengths to get themselves noticed.

Carson stripping to the Bonzo Dog Doo-Dah Band's 'Death Cab For Cutie') and the former United States Army Air Force base at West Malling Air Station where the glitzy make-believe ballroom sequence featuring The Beatles in white tie-and-tails performing 'Your Mother Should Know' took place in a vast disused aircraft hanger, while the 32 concrete anti-blast walls that had been erected to protect the aircraft based there during World War II, served as a futuristic backdrop for 'I Am The Walrus', with it's dancing policemen, eggmen and Lennon with a white rubber bathing cap pulled down to his ears. At the time, Lennon may have proclaimed himself to be the Walrus (goo goo g' joob), but years later added to the confusion by crooning "the Walrus was Paul". A sizeable amount of the production costs were poured into filming McCartney's 'Fool On The Hill' sequence on a rocky hillside high above Nice in the South of France during the last two days of October. Close to 90 percent of the ten hours of footage shot (including Stevie Winwood's group Traffic performing 'Here We Go Round The Mulberry Bush'), was dispensed with, resulting in the final print checking in at just 52 minutes duration.

While The Beatles frantically went about their *Magical Mystery Tour* assignment, Richard Lester was of the opinion that his professional association with The Beatles had run its natural course - but this was not to say that they wouldn't collaborate again sometime in the future should a suitable film property be acquired. **"I don't want to inhibit them [The Beatles] in any way, and I believe they should make their next film by themselves,"** he informed the *London Evening Standard's* Ray Connolly on 19 October 1967.

Richard Lester

'I think if I were to direct them again it would be a step backwards for them. I think they should go on and develop their talents in this field, and make a movie as they make their albums. I have a very great respect for The Beatles' talents and believe that they shouldn't be limited to the conventions of the professional film maker. I should be very happy to give technical advice as I am doing with their television film *Magical Mystery Tour*.'

The following day, Lester informed Michael Housego of the *Daily Sketch*, **"We sat down and talked about the next picture, and I think I should break away before we become too set in our ways. Their new picture together should be like the 'Sgt. Pepper' album which was one of their own creations and which grows on you. I don't think they should make another film with a professional film maker, but do it themselves and produce the world's most expensive home movie."**

And the world's most expensive home movie was precisely how *Magical Mystery Tour* was received by most people. The BBC anticipated that in its prime-time slot on Boxing Day (8.35 pm), *Magical Mystery Tour* would easily attract 20 million viewers and not the surprisingly low figure of 13 million. As the ratings revealed, an old movie featuring funny man Norman Wisdom and Honor Blackman, *The Square*

Peg was the most popular programme of the day (17 million), followed by *Top Of The Pops* (15 million), *(David) Frost Over Christmas* (14 million) and *Brigadoon* (13.5 million). Figures issued by TAM (Television Audience Measurement) estimated that *Magical Mystery Tour* was seen in 3,930,000 homes placing it in 25th position in popularity with Christmas viewers.

The critics deemed *Magical Mystery Tour* as being everything from 'witless rubbish' to 'colossal conceit' - a home movie of little merit. *Time* magazine commented, **"Paul directed, Ringo mugged, John did imitations, George danced a bit and, when the show hit the BBC last week, the audience gagged."** True to form, the Head of BBC 1, Paul Fox appeared oblivious to the torrent of criticism, insisting that it had been money well spent, but conceded, **"I agree it wasn't the easiest film to understand. I saw it four times and I began to understand it."** Comedian Nat Jackley - the Rubber Man, couldn't understand it full stop despite having participated: **"I thought it shocking. I couldn't make head or tail of it."**

The Beatles' million-dollar deal with NBC-TV was cancelled as a result of the critical battering that the British TV screening received. Only the soundtrack album really salvaged anything from the fiasco, but then Lennon's psychedelically ambiguous 'I Am The Walrus' had already caused a farrago before the screening for the line 'Boy, you've been a naughty girl you let your knickers down'. Though not subjected to an outright ban, BBC Radio chieftains had cautioned D-Js to avoid spinning this, the B-side to 'Hello Goodbye'.

Paul McCartney

'Everyone keeps preaching that the best way is to be 'open' when writing for teenagers. Then when we do we get criticised. Surely, the word 'knickers' can't offend anyone. Shakespeare wrote words a lot more naughtier than 'knickers'!'

John Lennon

'We chose the word because it is a lovely expressive word. It rolls off the tongue. It could mean anything!'

The minor controversy that surrounded 'I Am The Walrus' was in the past while the decision of Hong Kong to edit out Jan Carson's striptease sequence only warranted a one-liner. What needed redressing without any delay was the open hostility that had greeted *Magical Mystery Tour.* Within days, the movie's director, Paul McCartney quickly sprang to the defence:

Paul McCartney

'Was the film really so bad compared to the rest of Christmas TV ? You could hardly call the Queen's Speech a gasser! Our problem is that we are prisoners of our own fame. We could put on a moptop show, but we really don't like that sort of entertainment any more. Sure, we could have sung carols and done a first class Christmassy show starring The Beatles with lots of phoney tinsel like everybody else. It would have been the easiest thing in the world, but, we wanted to do something different. We thought we would do a fantasy film without a real plot. We thought the title was explanation enough. There was no plot and it was formless - deliberately so and those people expecting a plot were probably disappointed.'

'It was a magical tour. I didn't think if you went off into a fantasy you would have to spell it out. I didn't think you would need to come on the screen and say, "Right folks we are now going into the fantasy bit." We thought people would understand that it was 'magical' and a 'mystery tour.' We thought we would not underestimate people and would do something new. I know it wasn't the slickest job and may have looked a bit amateur, but it's better being controversial than purely boring. Obviously, we should have done it in a different way that everybody understood. Perhaps we should have had someone saying, "We are going magical now folks". We did not and the trouble is if people don't understand, they say "a load

> of old rubbish" and switch off. OK so maybe we boobed, maybe we didn't. The critics didn't like it, but plenty of friends did. We don't say it was a good film. It was our first attempt. It's like making a record. The first is never the best. If we goofed, then we goofed. It was a challenge and it didn't come off. We'll know better next time. If you watch it a second time it grows on you. This often happens when we make records.'

Magical Mystery Tour was screened again, on 5 January, this time in colour. But the damage had already been done. Nevertheless, the double EP-set-and-book had passed half-a-million units and overseas sales of the special were estimated to top one million pounds. In May a rumour did the rounds that suggested The Beatles were planning a sequel - this time it would be an invitation to an Edwardian picnic. The ever-cautious BBC stated they 'wouldn't commit ourselves to buying it without seeing it first!'

Almost three decades after the event, Paul McCartney is of the opinion that if they had by-passed television in favour of a cinema release, *Magical Mystery Tour* would have been received in quite a different manner to when it was premiered on Boxing Day.

BELOW The Beatles sample the local grass.

Paul McCartney

'Having said that, I'm not really sure how easy it would have been to do because it was made for television in the first place using 16mm film stock. I think it was really good and we all liked it at the time - it was a crazy thing and now it really looks good. But back in 1966, we showed it on TV in the Bruce Forsyth *(a British TV comedian and game-show host of long-standing popularity)* slot in black and white, which was not the way to show it. So you had all those Auntie Veras watching it and saying, 'Oh dear, I think those nice lads have all gone a bit funny!'

'At least it should have been screened late at night. It was good fun. Although we put on the credits, directed by The Beatles, by then I suppose I really was directing, but I had a bit of an inferiority complex about stepping out and saying, I directed this. But by and large I did direct it, so I had to take all the flack which I attempted to do. But take a look at it now, and it's quite a little classic for its time.'

MAGICAL MYSTERY TOUR

Apple Films

Director	The Beatles
Producer	The Beatles

CAST

John Lennon	
Paul McCartney	
George Harrison	
Ringo Starr	
Ivor Cutler	*Buster Bloodvessel*
Jessie Robbins	*Aunt Jessie*
Nat Jackley	*Happy Nat The Rubber Man*
Victor Spinetti	*Army Recruitment Sergeant*
The Bonzo Dog	
Doo-Dah Band	
Jan Carson	*The Stripper*
Derek Royale	*Jolly Jimmy Johnson*
	The Courier
George Caydon	*Little George*
	The Photographer
Mandy West	
Mal Evans	
Shirley	

Director	John Lennon Paul McCartney George Harrison Ringo Starr
Production Company	Apple Films
Producer	The Beatles
Time	55 minutes

MAGICAL MYSTERY TOUR

Parlophone MMT-1 (mono)
SMMT-1 (stereo)
Produced: George Martin
Released: December 1967

DISC ONE

A: Magical Mystery Tour (Paul)
Tuesday, 25 April
Wednesday, 26 April
Thursday, 27 April, 1967
Wednesday, 3 May, 1967

Your Mother Should Know (Paul)
Tuesday, 22 August
Wednesday, 23 August, 1967
Recorded Saturday, 16 September, 1967

B: I Am The Walrus (John)
Tuesday, 5 September, 1967

DISC TWO

A: The Fool On The Hill (Paul)
Monday, 25 September
Tuesday 26, September, 1967

Flying (instrumental)
Friday, 8 September, 1967

B: Blue Jay Way (George)
Wednesday, 6 September
Thursday, 7, September, 1967

US VERSION

Capitol MAL 2835 (mono)
SMAL 2835 (stereo)
Released: 27 November, 1967

SIDE ONE

1. **Magical Mystery Tour**
2. **The Fool On The Hill**
3. **Flying**
4. **Blue Jay Way**
5. **Your Mother Should Know**
6. **I Am The Walrus**

SIDE TWO

1. **Hello Goodbye** (Paul)
Monday, 2 October
Thursday, 19 October
Friday, 20 October
Wednesday, 25 October
Thursday, 2 November, 1967

2 **Strawberry Fields Forever** (John)
Thursday, 24 November, 1966
Monday, 28 November, 1966
Tuesday, 29 November, 1966
Thursday, 8 December, 1966
Friday, 9 December, 1966
Thursday, 15 December, 1966
Wednesday, 21 December, 1966

3 **Penny Lane** (Paul)
Thursday, 29 December, 1966
Friday, 30 December, 1966
Thursday, 5 January, 1967
Friday, 6 January, 1967
Monday, 9 January, 1967
Tuesday, 10 January, 1967
Thursday, 12 January, 1967
Tuesday, 17 January, 1967

4 **Baby You're A Rich Man** (John)
dropped from soundtrack album but used in movie
Thursday, 1 May, 1967

5 **All You Need Is Love** (John)
Sunday, 25 June, 1967

UK 45s

A: Hello, Goodbye
B: I Am The Walrus
Parlophone R5655
Released: 24 November, 1967

US 45s

A: Hello, Goodbye
B: I Am The Walrus
Capitol 2056
Released: 27 November, 1967

Production note:
Two instrumental compositions, the first by Lennon & McCartney, the second, attributed to all four members, were recorded for 'Magical Mystery Tour' and used exclusively as incidental music on the soundtrack.

'Shirley's Wild Accordion'
Thursday, October 12, 1967
featuring Shirley Evans (accordion), Reg Wale (piano) plus Paul and Ringo

'Jessie's Dream' (instrumental)
no recording date
The Beatles

The Bonzo Dog Doo-Dah Band performed their own composition **'Death Cab For Cutie'** in a Soho Strip Club sequence.

ABOVE FROM LEFT TO RIGHT Various versions of the single *'Hello, Goodbye'*: UK export (for Denmark) version, Danish version and Spanish version.

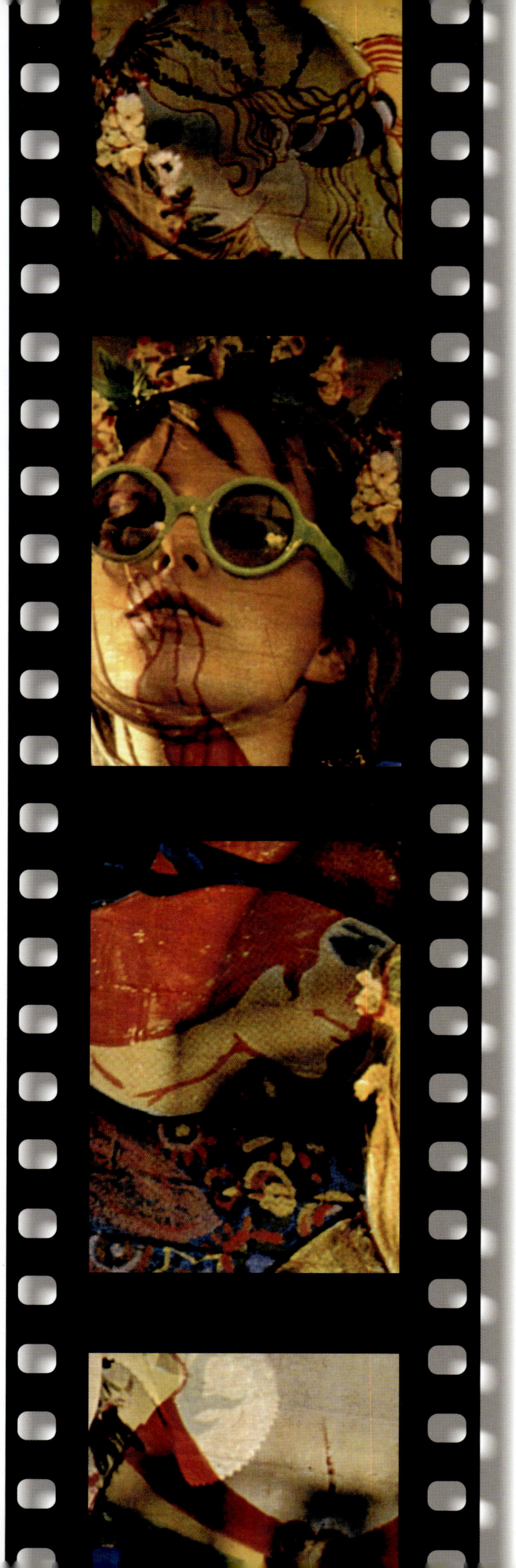

14

POOR OSCAR
HE ONLY
WANTED TO
WATCH HER
THROUGH THE
WONDERWALL

WONDERWALL

The soundtrack to *Wonderwall* launched Apple Records on 1 November, 1968 - just days before the release of The Beatles' own 'White Album'. Though Harrison doesn't actually perform on any of the tracks, it still amounted to the first official solo project by one of the Fabs. Recorded, both at Abbey Road and EMI's studio in Bombay, during November 1967 and January 1968, Harrison's exotic score featured a total of 13 local soundtrack musicians including sarod maestro Ashish Khan and famed flautist Hari Prasad Chaurasia - the latter known for having the flesh between his fingers surgically expanded so as to allow him to play specially carved flutes.

It was at one of these sessions that Harrison also taped the instrumental backing track for a future Beatle release 'The Inner Light'.

As to the movie: plot-wise *Wonderwall* is of the hippy-drippy variety that amounts to a voyeuristic experience revolving around the antics of an absent-minded scientist who, when peeping through a hole in an adjoining wall, bares silent witness to the shenanigans of his photographic-model neighbour Penny (Jane Birkin).

BELOW The *'Wonderwall'* soundtrack LP. This was the first release by Apple.

BELOW George and Patti dressed to thrill.

WONDERWALL

Alan Clore Films

Director	Joe Massot
Producer	Andrew Braunsberg

CAST

Jack MacGowran:	Oscar Collins
Jane Birkin:	Penny
Irene Handl:	Mrs. Peurofoy
Richard Wattis:	Perkins
Iain Quarrier:	Young Man
Beatrix Lehmann:	Mother
Brian Walsh:	Photographer
Sean Lynch:	Riley
Bee Duffell:	Mrs. Charmer
Noel Trevarthen:	Policeman
Genevieve:	Girl with leaflet
Sonia Dean:	Teacher
Suki Poitier:	Other Girl

CREDITS

Director	Joe Massot
Production Company	Alan Clore Films
Producer	Andrew Braunsberg
Production Manager	Ed Harper
Assistant Director	Jonathan Benson
Scriptwriter	Guillermo Cain
Original Story	Gerard Brach
Cinematography	Harry Waxman
Editor	Rusty Coppleman
Art Director	Assheton Gorton
Music	George Harrison
Costumes	Jocelyn Rickards
Sound	Laurie Clarkson
Length	8260 feet (2518 metres)
Running Time	92 minutes

15

The Film That Never Was: FOUR

JOE ORTON'S *'UP AGAINST IT'*

'The whole idea of making films is good. Not big expensive films, but films you make because you fancy making a film. When you're kids, you say, lets play a game - but when you've got money to do things like play games...well almost - you can do the same things you did as a kid.'
Paul McCartney

M*agical Mystery Tour* having been given a universal thumbs down and the full-length animated *Yellow Submarine* still in production, The Beatles were looking for suitable big screen properties. At this juncture in their fledgling movie career, The Beatles wanted a unique vehicle, something that would reflect their tastes. They had done the 'lovable moptops' scenario twice and, as their music revealed, it was definitely time to move on. Back in 1963, during the first flush of Beatlemania, Paul McCartney had attempted to explain the roots of The Beatles' humour which, in the cold light of day, was similar to that commonly shared by school kids everywhere.

Paul McCartney
'Our humour is based upon anything else that other people don't laugh at. Death for instance or disease - it sounds dreadful if you write it down, but it's the cruelties, the cruel stuff that makes us laugh.'

So, it was easy to see why they would be easily attracted to the kind of black comedy farce that was at the root of such Joe Orton plays as *The Ruffian On The Stairs, Loot* and *Entertaining Mr Sloane.* The Beatles, as much as anyone, could identify with the sheer speed of Orton's success and the controversial shock waves it made. It was as meteoric as any pop star's, and, as the tragic events soon to be played out dictated, it was to be brutally snuffed out just as quickly. But that was still in the future.

Richard Lester
'I think that they were interested in playing around with film-making themselves, but knew that it probably wouldn't satisfy United Artists. By this time, they were already being pulled in four separate directions.

Furthermore, they more or less had decided that they no longer wanted to tour. There wasn't a great enthusiasm for saying we're going to carry on a long career of film-making - like Elvis Presley, we're going to make a film a year because that's what we do as part of our life. That certainly wasn't the case with The Beatles. I think they now regarded making films as an obligation.'

'They (The Beatles) were prepared to be dark because John was willing to appear in a very dark film for me - *How I Won The War*. I don't believe that they ever worried about image - they were much too smart for that.'

In the same manner as a proven writer like Alun Owen had been chosen to write *A Hard Day's Night*, following the good-natured knockabout that was *Help!* The Beatles were again looking for a writer of substance and reputation. John Kinsley 'Joe' Orton, who had been born in Leicester on New Year's Day 1933, seemed to be the most likely candidate for the role. On the question of being perceived as slightly more serious than some people regarded them, The Beatles' albeit brief association with Orton was a tentative step in such a direction.

Paul McCartney
'Around about those times, I was living in London whereas the others were out in Weybridge, Surrey and places like that and so I saw a lot of theatre. In the process, I was introduced to the National Theatre and stuff like that. Eventually, I got to know a lot of people on that scene and hung out with some of them. Even when I was living up in Liverpool, I used to go the Royal Court Theatre on my own and sit up in the gods (balcony) and think of myself as a budding director or playwright. I also read a lot of plays like *Salome*, the works of Oscar Wilde, George Bernard Shaw and so many others like that. I also happened to have a brilliant teacher who had been educated at Oxford. And it was he who turned me right on to this kind of stuff. So I was very much into plays and playwrights and I knew people like Harold Pinter.'

'I was also a backer for the original stage production of Joe Orton's *Loot* - an 'angel'...put a thousand pounds into it. That was one of my great excitements. To be truthful, I was quite besotted by the theatre. It was all so very cool...all very vital. I used to attend a lot of the

"With its political assassination, guerrilla warfare and transvestism, it (*Up Against It*) might have been designed with The Beatles in mind."
Joe Orton

more radical productions. You'd often see me at the Royal Court Theatre...I also enjoyed things like the *Footlights Revue* where I'd see David Frost and Peter Cook and Dudley Moore...all these boys coming down from Cambridge and performing in pubs.'

'A lot of the time I also used to go to The Establishment Club in Greek Street which was run by Peter Cook. Living in St John's Wood I was virtually five minutes away from the very centre of London and everything that was happening on that scene. Outside of what I was doing with The Beatles my life was full of that kind of thing and, of course, I was going out with an actress at the time (Jane Asher).'

From December 1966 right up until August 1967, Joe Orton maintained a series of highly detailed personal diaries. On Thursday, 12 January, 1967, Orton wrote this entry:

A man called Walter Shenson called Peggy (Peggy Ramsay, his agent). He is the man who produced the first two Beatles' films. He had a script written by somebody else. It isn't quite good enough. *'Dull'*, he said, "would you like to see it with a view to working on the film script?" I was very impressed by this, but I put on a nonchalant manner. Well, I'm frightfully up to my eyes in it at the moment, I said, I'm writing my third play. "I'd certainly love you to take a look at this draft", he said, "I've discussed it with the *'boys'*...I mean, I mentioned your name to them...they've heard of you!" By this time I was feeling foolish and not at all nonchalant. "'Er yes," I said, "'Er, please send the script over and I'll read it."

The following Monday (16 January), Shenson casually informed Joe Orton that a remake of the Alexander Dumas classic, *The Three Musketeers* had been on the short list of possible Beatles movies. Brigitte Bardot no less, insisted Shenson, had been approached for the role of the wicked Lady De Winter. However, The Beatles had vetoed the idea. It was also on this day, that Orton gave his script the title *Up Against It*. What Orton didn't tell Shenson, or anyone else for that matter, was that *Up Against It* had first began life as a novel, *The Silver Bucket*. Written as far back as 1953, it was Orton's first collaboration with Kenneth Halliwall, his lover for 16 years. For the *Up Against It* script Orton fused *The Silver Bucket* with elements from what became his last novel *The Vision Of Gombold Proval* which he wrote in 1961. It would be published after his death as *Head To Toe*.

Writing in his Diary, that day, Orton revealed:

> **Miss Drumgoole and Father Brodie have come to life as interesting characters. Which should delight The Beatles. I'm not bothering to write characters for them. I shall just do all my box of tricks - SLOANE and HAL on them. After all if I repeat myself in this film it doesn't matter. Nobody who sees the film will have seen (Entertaining Mr.)SLOANE or LOOT.**

On the Wednesday (18th), Shenson telephoned Orton stating Brian Epstein was 'delighted' that Orton had agreed to write the movie. In truth, Orton saw his involvement with The Beatles as money for old rope and instructed Peggy Ramsay to ask for £15,000, but nothing lower than £10,000. Ramsay said, she'd be pleased with £12,000 and a percentage. Orton's last word on the matter was that if they said no, to £10,000 **'they can fuck themselves.'** Orton himself casually brought up the question of money when invited, by Epstein, to meet Paul McCartney on the 24th.

As he re-worked elements of *Head To Toe* into this 'new' script, Orton mused that, **"with its political assassination, guerrilla warfare and transvestism - it might have been designed with the Beatles in mind!"** Though no legal contracts had as yet been presented for signing, by way of a gesture of goodwill, Walter Shenson paid Orton £5,000 for the first draft. If The Beatles rejected *Up Against It,* Shenson explained, Orton could buy back his manuscript.

Aware of the unorthodoxly of Orton's work, Shenson was mindful that the project shouldn't reflect the lovable moptops in an unflattering manner; and went on about how the Fabs were role models to young people the world over and their actions emulated by their fans. Whether or not he had studied Orton's first draft of *Up Against It* carefully or just passed it on is open to question, but it would seem that Shenson was unaware of the subversiveness of what Orton was writing. If he had connected, he certainly didn't let on.

> **I hadn't the heart to tell him,** wrote Orton, on 11 February , **that the boys, in my script, have been caught in-flagrant, become involved in dubious political activity, dressed as women, committed murder, been put in prison and committed adultery.**

Or, that at the end of the plot, the Fabs would all end up in bed with one woman (Miss Drumgoole) before diving under the sheets!

Orton delivered the first draft on 25 February. Previous to this, McTurk's character had been split into four actors, all of whom answered to the same name. For this updated version Orton had written them as separate characters: Ian McTurk, Christopher Low and Jack Ramsay. Oscar Lewenstein, who had co-produced *Loot* at both the Cochrane and Criterion Theatres, was the first person to read the script and wholeheartedly approved of

ABOVE Joe Orton simultaneously being the toast and the enfant terrible of London's West-End Theatreland.

its content. Lewenstein went so far as to inform Orton that it was probably the best first draft he'd ever read. Praise indeed from someone whose impressive list of production credits included *Tom Jones, A Taste Of Honey* and *The Loneliness Of The Long Distance Runner.*

As events revealed, Orton's work wasn't well received elsewhere. And, despite his dairy entries, those close to the project believe that, in reality, Orton himself never seriously expected that The Beatles would accept his script in its original form. It would have been hard to image John, Paul, George and Ringo being at ease with the extremely dark and sexually ambiguous plot of Orton's anarchic comedy. The bottom line was that *Up Against It,* as a Beatles' project, was not acceptable and could possibly inflict irrevocable damage to their reputation.

Richard Lester
'I don't think that it would have worked at all. I don't think they possessed the acting skills to deal with those linguistic acrobatics that Orton demanded. It's a very specialised kind of work and I think that you cannot jump into that when the only thing that you had done up until this point was to play themselves with a rough-and-ready charm. Everything I have ever seen of Joe Orton's requires an enormous amount of vocal dexterity and discipline which I honestly feel would have been hard for them to achieve at this stage in their career.'

Orton completed *Up Against It* towards the end of February. On the last day of the month the film rights for *Loot* were sold for a reported £100,000. During the first week of April, the script of *Up Against It* was returned to Orton without the courtesy of an explanation and a deafening silence from Brian Epstein's office. The story leaked into the papers with the 10 April edition of the *London Evening Standard* stating that the incident had proved to be a 'shock to Joe Orton's pride.' However, in just two days, the whole incident was turned around when Oscar Lewenstein bought the rights to *Up Against It* for £10,000 plus ten percent of future production profits.

Paul McCartney
'The reason why we didn't do *Up Against It* wasn't because it was too far out or anything like that. We didn't do it because it was gay. We weren't gay and really that was all there was to it. It was quite simple, really. Brian was gay...and so he and the gay crowd could appreciate it. Now, it wasn't that we were anti-gay - just that we, The Beatles, weren't gay.'

As to the question whether The Beatles secretly felt that to appear in *Up Against It* would ruin or at least partially harm their career?

Paul McCartney
'I don't know about that...I don't know if that would be the case. We just didn't like being put in that kind of a bag...it would have been like having us play Romany gypsies. So, it would be strange for us playing something we weren't - and we weren't gay. Joe Orton was great...I liked him a lot as a person...but I was in a very funny mood then. I remember having lunch with Joe round at Brian's house and trying to get a handle on it all...attempting to give him some idea where we were at. When I look back on it now, I remember making a terrible faux pas. I said, "I'm not really into words, Joe", which was a really strange thing for me to say to a playwright like Orton who was known for writing very wordy plays. But he understood what I meant.'

Though previously Richard Lester hadn't been involved when it had been created as a Beatle property, he now found himself being asked to transfer *Up Against It* into big screen vehicle.

Richard Lester
'We had a deal to prepare a version of that screen play, but altered it so that instead of The Beatles, it would be Rolling Stone Mick Jagger and (yet-to-be-knighted) actor Ian McKellen plus two girls. In essence, the plan was to now turn it into a musical film.'

Beatle music at Joe Orton cremation

DAILY TELEGRAPH REPORTER

BEATLES music was played yesterday at the funeral of Joe Orton, author of the West End play "Loot."

The service started with "A Day in the Life" from the Beatles' record, "Sergeant Pepper's Lonely Hearts Club Band." It was Orton's favourite tune.

The unusual opening to an unusual cremation ceremony was in keeping with Orton's "black comedy" writing. A coffin was the main "prop" in "Loot."

Orton, 34, was an atheist, which set the tone for the service in the West Chapel of the Golders Green Crematorium. Donald Pleasence, the actor, read a "Hilarium Memoriam" to a subdued gathering which included members of Joe Orton's family and the cast of "Loot."

"Hilarity in death"

The "Hilarium" mirrored Orton's life, attitudes, and beliefs:

Some met together
when he died,
Not in the name of any God,
But in his name—
Whom They lost to the coffin
when the box which caused
his endless mirth,
His Lesson which he could
not read again.
Hilarity in death,
And now his censored spirit
in oblivion—free.
Perhaps it's hard to see that
he'd have thought it funny
—mad.
They will not weep for him,
They know that if they did
He'd think they'd missed
the joke.
The joke that some would say
was "in bad taste,"
And others who are calmer
"just a waste,"
They will not weep for him
No one will see their tears
No weeping could be heard and
any way he knew except
in them.
He wouldn't now be anywhere.
When calm and humour clear
their grief,
Then love for him must turn
all pain to laughter
Not despair.

Paul McCartney

'I could have seen where that might have worked...Mick is a little bit more on the gay side, so I guess he would be happier with that. *Up Against It* needed that. It needed a bit of effeminacy or whatever ...needed a little bit of what Joe and his mate were to make it live. You just can't stick some butch guys in there from Liverpool who don't get it. That was the problem if we had decided to go with it...we wouldn't have got it. It really needed somebody who'd got it, to make it work.'

The project immediately ran into difficulty when trying to find a writer capable of adapting Orton's unique style of writing. Roger McGough and Charles Wood were among those asked to prepared two or three pages to ascertain whether or not they were compatible.

Richard Lester

'It never worked. Joe's was such a unique voice that the writers threw up their hands and agreed it was impossible to successfully blend their work with his without it becoming clumsy.'

That idea was abandoned for the time being. On the morning of 9 August, 1967, a chauffeur-driven limousine was sent to Joe Orton's flat at 25 Noel Road in North London, with instructions to transport him to Twickenham Studios for a meeting with producer Oscar Lewenstein and director Richard Lester. The intention was to discuss Orton's *Up Against It* script. At the same time, Orton was finishing off the final rewrite for his next play *What The Butler Saw*. Upon arrival at Orton's address, the chauffeur discovered a horrific, some would say Ortonesque, scene of carnage.

In the early hours of that morning, it appears that a violent argument erupted between Joe Orton and the increasingly mentally unstable Kenneth Halliwell. Having viciously caved in the head of his 34-year old lover with nine frenzied hammer blows, the naked and distraught Halliwell washed down 22 Nembutal tablets with a glass of tinned grapefruit juice. According to police doctors, 41-year old Halliwell took less than 30 seconds to die. Ironically, the fatally wounded Orton may have lingered slightly longer. Halliwell had left a brief note.

If you read his dairy all will be explained. KH
P.S. Especially the latter part.

The funeral of Joe Orton took place at the Golders Green Crematorium on Friday, 18 August, 1967. During the brief service, Orton's favourite record was played - The Beatles' 'A Day In the Life'. Just nine days later (Sunday, 27 August), Brian Epstein was found dead in tragic circumstances, aged 32. His existing contract with The Beatles had but six weeks left to run.

FOOTNOTE:

'The Orton Diaries' Edited by John Lahr and published by Minerva

JOE ORTON OUTSIDE HIS FLAT

£100,000 'Loot' author found dead

By HARRY LONGMUIR

JOE ORTON, the bed-sitter playwright who became obsessed by death and made a fortune writing about it, died violently yesterday.

The 34-year-old author of the West End hit play *Loot* was found battered to death in his top-floor flat in Noel Road, Islington, London, N. Later police took away a hammer.

Near him was the body of his close friend, 41-year-old Kenneth Halliwell. He is believed to have died from a drug overdose. The two men shared the flat for six years.

They were found by Mr. Derek Taylor, 38-year-old chauffeur employed by a film promoter. Mr. Taylor was told to take Orton to studios at Twickenham for discussions about a film the author had been commissioned to write.

When he arrived at the flat Mr. Taylor got no reply. He looked through the letterbox and saw Halliwell lying on the hall floor.

A police doctor and senior detectives were at the flat for more than five hours. There were signs of a violent struggle. Orton was in pyjamas. Halliwell partly dressed.

Orton was paid £100,000 for the film rights of *Loot*. Its main prop is a coffin. Last night the show went on as usual at the Criterion.

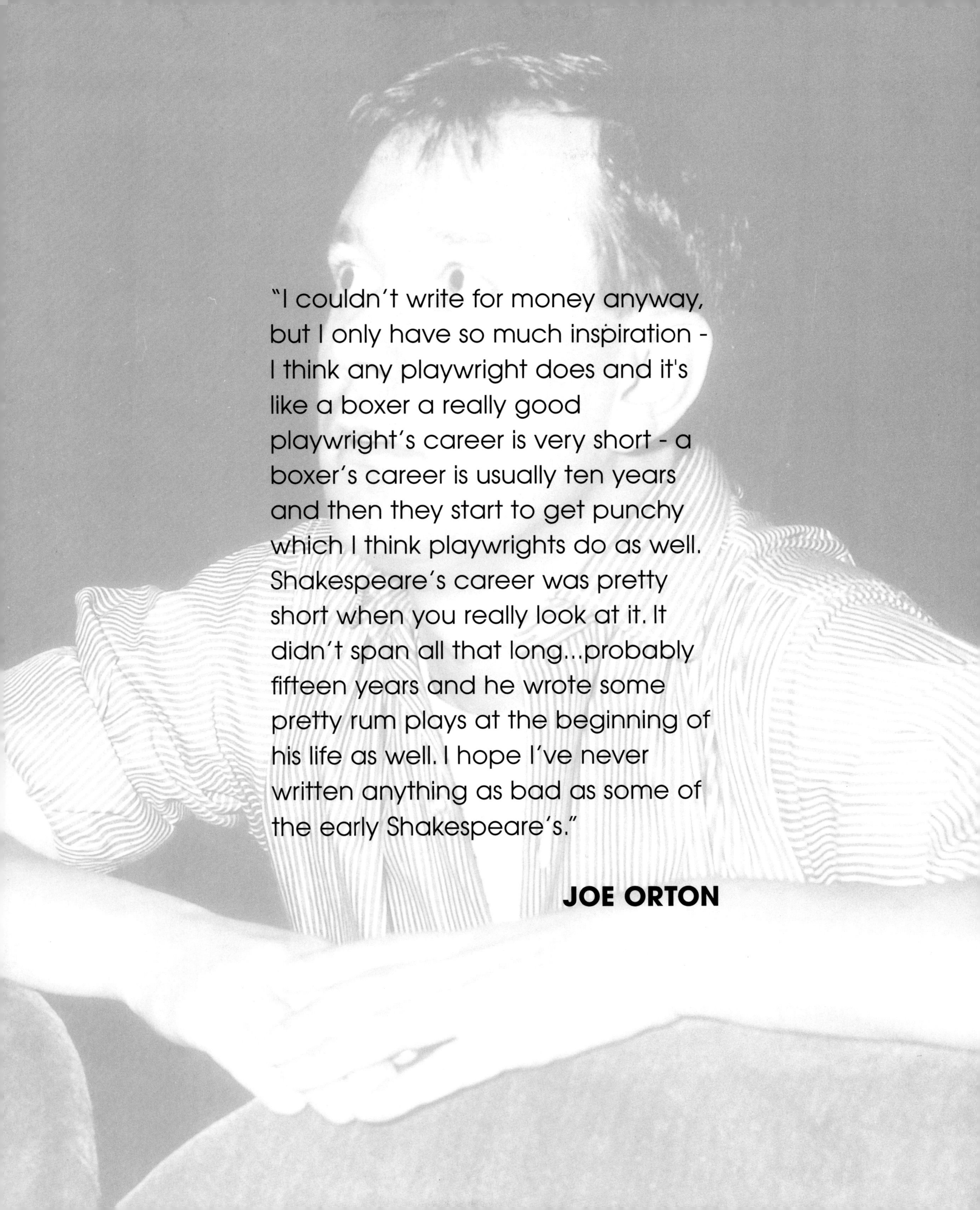

"I couldn't write for money anyway, but I only have so much inspiration - I think any playwright does and it's like a boxer a really good playwright's career is very short - a boxer's career is usually ten years and then they start to get punchy which I think playwrights do as well. Shakespeare's career was pretty short when you really look at it. It didn't span all that long...probably fifteen years and he wrote some pretty rum plays at the beginning of his life as well. I hope I've never written anything as bad as some of the early Shakespeare's."

JOE ORTON

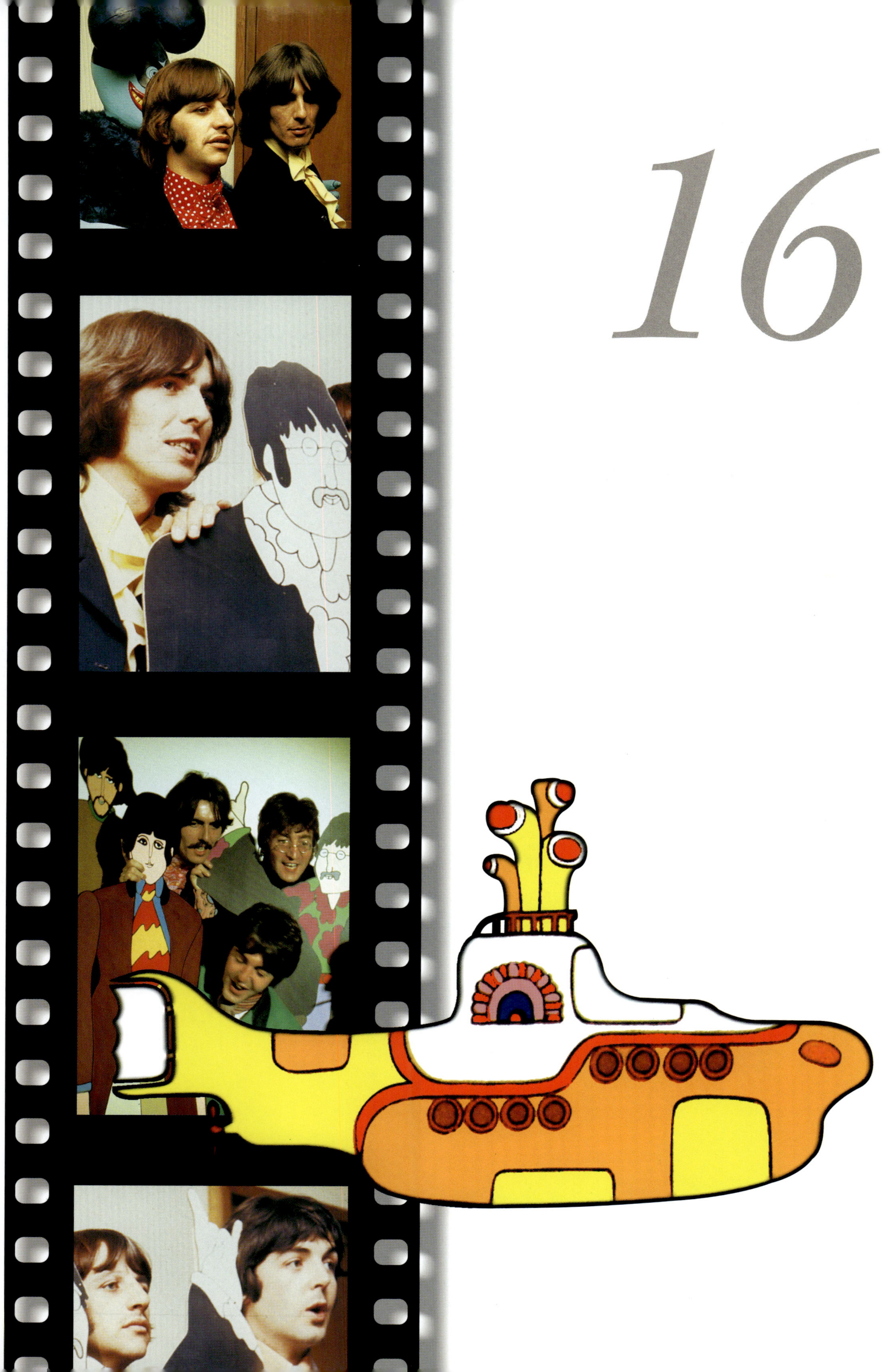

16

YELLOW SUBMARINE

Once upon a time...or maybe twice...there was an unearthly paradise called...PEPPERLAND. So began *Yellow Submarine.* The Beatles were not so much facing the 'difficult' third album syndrome which is often the most arduous test for any rock group shooting for the big one. In their case what was to become *Yellow Submarine* was merely a means to an end. And the end in question was the fulfilment of their three picture deal with United Artists. As such, it was no longer a major priority.

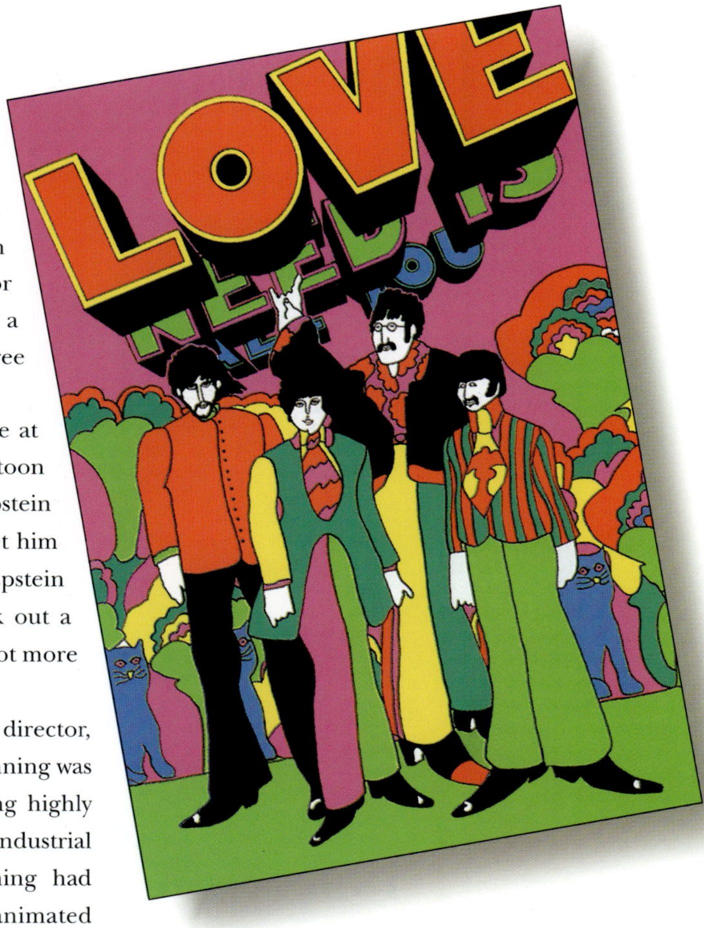

Two years earlier, Al Brodax (a one-time professor of classic literature at Yale known for his pushy demeanour) produced 39 episodes of a Beatles cartoon series for ABC-TV and ever since then had perpetually hounded Brian Epstein (whom he looked upon as a 'brilliant but very miserable son-of-a-bitch') to let him make a full-length animated version for cinema release. Reluctantly, Epstein eventually capitulated and Brodax scooted off to New Hampshire to knock out a screen play with Erich Segal who pocketed $16,000 for his effort - but a whole lot more when he later penned his best selling confectionery *Love Story.*

First, an experienced team of animators was assembled by the film's director, George Dunning who had previously worked on the Beatles TV cartoons. Dunning was a Canadian whose London-based production company specialised in making highly lucrative advertising commercials plus films for educational, corporate and industrial purposes. Avoiding traditional Disney-esque animation techniques, Dunning had earlier experimented with the avant-garde (*The Apple*), switching to animated watercolours (*The Flying Man*) before his research into a more pictorial approach led him into the realms of psychedelia with *Yellow Submarine.* A creative magpie, Dunning filled *Yellow Submarine* with numerous direct references to Sixties Pop Art and the hallucinatory rainbow of psychedelia. It was scriptwriter Lee Minoff's idea of using one of The Beatles' hits as a basis for the story.

To create the cast of animated characters, Dunning hired the services of German graphic artist Heinz Edelmann, whose innovative deployment of abstract light-show psychedelics, paisley pop art imagery and Beardsley derived decoratives had already been seized upon by leading advertising design studios. Inspiration was plucked from the most unusual sources: an indigestible Turkish meal gave Edelmann the idea to create The Snapping Turtle Turks, while the Chief Blue Meanie had movements culled from wartime Hitler newsreels. Indeed, 'treated' film footage was utilised throughout *Yellow Submarine* - a technique later pursued elsewhere in the making of a star-crossed animated version of *The Lord Of The Rings.*

Yellow Submarine was completed in one year, using a hard-working team of 40 animators and 140 technical artists who turned Edelmann's original sketches into half a million completed pictures.

'Eighty thousand leagues beneath the sea it lay...or lied, I'm not too sure...'

The flimsy plot to *Yellow Submarine* has the Blue Meanies (the enemies of joy, colour and music) invading tranquil Pepperland and setting up a harsh dictatorship.The extent of the evil that pervades the Blue Meanies is reflected when their leader, upon hearing the joyous sounds of Sgt Pepper's Band, remarks **'Music as foul as a day in Spring.'** Thereafter, the Blue Meanies - supported by the Flying Glove, the Apple Bonkers and the Count Down Clown - launch an anti-music missile attack (**'A world without music is a Blue world'**), against the Lord Mayor and the inhabitants of Pepperland. When these are hit by the Meanies' Blue Splotch, they are drained of colour, turn grey-black and freeze in an awkward position.

Old Fred, the orchestra conductor, manages to escape to the 'upper world' in the Yellow Submarine. There he locates John, Paul, George and Ringo in Penny Lane and convinces them to return with him, in the Yellow Submarine, to Pepperland. Together they head for the Sea of Green but first they have to navigate through the adventure-

ABOVE Some 'Yellow Submarine' writing paper.

BELOW Max, one of the dreaded Blue Meanies.

filled Seas of Music, Cinema, Personalities (aka Sea of Time), Phrenology, Science and Holes. Along the way, they befriend Boob (The Nowhere Man). Having reached Pepperland, the Foursome recapture the musical instruments originally confiscated by the Blue Meanies and in the ensuing battle, defeat and drive off the invaders. Peace and happiness and glorious colour is once more restored to Pepperland and marked by a celebratory Victory Concert.

The actual 'Yellow Submarine' script was littered with schoolboyish puns and throwaway one-liners, all of which were a sea mile away from the barbed wit of 'A Hard Day's Night'. For example:

Paul
'I feel a song comin' on.'
John
'Well fight it off.'
George
'Want a bite of my cotton candy?'
Ringo
'Nah, disappears when you eat it. Melts before you ever taste it.'

The visual jokes were more plentiful and infinitely more amusing. At one point, George is transformed into the Pink Panther. In the Sea of Cinema sequence, the soundtrack fills with the strains of 'Lucy In The Sky With Diamonds' as, in rapid succession, we see Ringo caught in the crossfire between Red Indians and the US Cavalry; Paul involved in a World War I aerial dogfight; George dodging a naval battle fought by the forces of the USA and Japan. This and other bizarre enactments is followed by sequences that include King Kong, The Sheik, a cops and robbers shootout, Moses, Cicero, Shakespeare, Napoleon, Freud, Alberts Einstein and Schweitzer, Quasimodo and so on.

ABOVE A *'Yellow Submarine'* alarm clock, one of the many pieces of film merchandise that were made.

BELOW "I didn't feel that the characters were very well drawn...and of course we still had those terrible - *'Hello George', 'Hello Paul'* - those dreadful bloody voices."
Paul McCartney

George Dunning

'The film, apart from story and plot, was designed as an 'experience'. Feature film audiences want this 'sensation' or 'experience'. Since the film was made of drawings and paintings, we decided to bring in all the images familiar to the popular mind that we could. My opinion about long or short animated films is complex. Many subjects, ideas and designs have limited quantities for a general audience, and therefore the film should be limited or short as well. The artistic validity of long animated films is often a question of their relative vulgarity. Distributors give backing to vulgar films. In the last year (1971) I have made a three-minute film *Damon The Mover*. This demonstrates that I still believe in short films.'

'It is always a joy to work on a film which is worth making. This standard of 'worth making' eliminates most films we see. The public is forever optimistic, and when it sees a film that was worth while they are quite ready to forget all the bad films they have seen before.'

If *A Hard Day's Night* and *Help!* had successfully perpetuated The Beatles' myth far beyond anyone's wildest expectations, then *Yellow Submarine* depicted the Fabs as an environmentally friendly aquarian Fantastic Four with an all-you-need-is-love philosophy rather than violently pulverising their opponents into oblivion. A generation later, they would probably have taken on the guise of chop-socky Martial Art(s)-ists!

United Artists' executives may have failed to brow-beat Richard Lester into erasing The Beatles' original voice track to *A Hard Day's Night* and redubbing it with mid-Atlantic voices, but Brodax achieved this from the moment *Yellow Submarine* was put into production. But then, it was never Brodax's intention to use the real voices of the Fab Four from the outset. Neither was such a project ever on the foursome's agenda. Allegedly, Brodax didn't have much truck with the group. Ringo he unkindly termed a 'clutz' and McCartney 'a wise-ass'. However, upon the movie's release, even close Beatle-watchers and critics alike were under the impression that the voices they were hearing were the genuine article. However, by the time it went into production, any enthusiasm The Beatles had for *Yellow Submarine* had quickly evaporated as their newly founded business empire - Apple Corp in Savile Row took priority over all else.

ABOVE Yet another bit of film merchandise in the form of a *Yellow Submarine* watch.

ABOVE The sheet music for *'Hey Bulldog'*, one of the new songs written specifically for *Yellow Submarine.*

Similarly, creating new material - even something as minimal as four songs - wasn't something that easily distracted The Beatles. So it wasn't surprising that they somewhat distanced themselves from the project. However, half-way through production, The Beatles liked some of what they saw and agreed to the very briefest of cameo appearances at the very end of the film. In truth, the terms of the contract allowed King Features the rights to use up to a dozen existing Beatle songs to accompany the on-screen action, but also promised four new titles which The Beatles hoped to release on a seven-inch EP. They turned out to be:

Only A Northern Song
Monday, 13 and Tuesday, 14 February, 1967
Thursday 20 & Friday 21, April, 1967

It's All Too Much
Thursday, 25 and Friday, 26 May, 1967
Friday, 2 June , 1967

All Together Now
Friday, 12 May, 1967

Hey Bulldog (John)
Sunday, 11 February, 1968

Consequently, a production master comprising (Side One) 'Only A Northern Song', 'Hey Bulldog' plus the as-yet-unreleased 'Across The Universe', (Side Two) 'All Together Now' and 'It's All Too Much' was prepared for the pressing plant. That was until it was quickly brought to The Beatles' attention, that, Stateside, where their product enjoyed maximum sales, Extended Play records were no longer acceptable vinyl currency. As a result, 'Across The Universe' was put back into cold storage and the four new songs in question were hastily bolted together with the already available title track and 'All You Need Is Love' to make up side one of a soon-to-be-released album.

'Only A Northern Song' and 'It's All Too Much' came from George: the former track was originally shortlisted for 'Sgt Pepper', but had been benched in favour of 'Within You, Without You.' 'All Together Now', sung by Paul, was knocked together in just one evening, as was John's contribution 'Hey Bulldog'. Surprisingly, 'Hey Bulldog' was edited out of all but a few prints of 'Yellow Submarine'. George Martin's incidental orchestral material accounted for Side Two. Obligatory soundtrack albums didn't come easier.

It has been suggested The Beatles' cameo appearance right at the end of the film had to do with meeting contractual obligations. The fact that they actually appear in person fulfiled their required participation. *Yellow Submarine* proved to be a ground-breaking exercise for its ability to attract mixed audiences of young adults and children. It quickly proved to be an inspiration to other production companies to sharpen their pencils and break out the paintbox when, prior to *Yellow Submarine*, they had fought shy of venturing into the realm of feature-length animation where only Disney seemed able to profit at the box office.

The film premiered in July 1968. *Time* magazine reported: **"If the result seems less a coherent story than a two-hour pot high, *Yellow Submarine* is still a break through of the feature film and art's intimacy with the unconscious."** For the first time in years, not only was this a film that attracted both the adult and kid dollar, but it offered a new and 'hip' style of animation which could be appreciated on many (cosmic) levels. The inviting smell of hot buttered popcorn mingled with more exotic herbal aromas in many a darkened cinema. It continued to do so for years to come when *Yellow Submarine* joined *Easy Rider, Performance, Five Easy Pieces, Woodstock, Alice's Restaurant* and similar repertory material on the midnight matinee Art House circuit.

Everyone having had their say, to what extent were The Beatles actually involved in the *Yellow Submarine* project?

Paul McCartney

'I'm a great fan of animation and really love all those films that come out of the Disney studios. It's all extremely clever and highly skillful. And, like the Superman comics, I'm convinced that all those illustrators are true artists, and, as such, I've always had a great admiration for them. King Features did the Beatles cartoon series for TV which I have to state, we didn't really like. To be honest, we all thought it was a joke and consequently we refused to do the voices for it. But still, we realised that it was something that would maybe add to our popularity and it was a bit of a kids deal for us - we were a little bit more grown-up than that. Financially, it was a good deal and would make a lot of money...and the kids seem to like it. It wasn't anything we were madly against, but at the same time we weren't really keen on the people from King. They were nice enough people, but artistically we really weren't that impressed.'

'Al Brodax talked to us about the possibility of doing a feature and we met at my house in London. Erich Segal came along as well. I was keen to do something and said, we could get like a Disney thing going - but even better, it could be fantastic and I talked to them about my song, *Yellow Submarine* which they wanted to build the film around. Anyway, I told them that I had very definite thoughts about this...there is a land of actual submarines - all different coloured and in fact it's a commune. And, there's the old guy who sails to sea and talks to people when he's on the beach and so, if we're going to do a full-length animated movie, then it should be this wonderful Disneyesque adventure, only a little bit more far out; basically follow the story of the song and then enlarge upon it.'

ABOVE Along with the popularity of The Beatles came the popularity of collectable cigarette and bubble gum cards.

'At the start, all four of us hoped for something a little bit groovier...sort of more classic *Pinocchio* or *Snow White*...I thought that we could get more

into those kind of realms...really get into making this something of a much more exciting, classic animated movie. Right away, they made it clear that they weren't keen to do just a straight Disney thing...said, "we think you're further out now"...so from being rather childish - which that cartoon series most definitely was, they wanted to go completely psychedelic! So they went ahead and made something that, at the time, I wasn't wild about because it lacked the ingenuity and the warmth and the overall magic you associate with Disney. The end result was that *Yellow Submarine* just didn't draw me into it. Basically, I thought it was a lot of very clever sequences but nothing more. Looking back on it now, it most definitely is a piece of its time and you can't escape the fact that it was very innovative.'

'I don't mind it as much now as I did back then. I didn't feel that the characters were very well drawn...they were a little bit silly. And, of course, we still had those terrible 'Hello George', 'Hello Paul' - those dreadful, bloody voices. For me, *Yellow Submarine* is a bit like *Magical Mystery Tour* - a bit disappointing at the time but now it looks a lot better.'

Whatever their individual reservations, all four Beatles turned up for the Premiere on 17 July, 1968. Despite doing capacity box-office business at the London Pavilion (taking £7,000 a week), the Rank Organisation did not give *Yellow Submarine* a full general release throughout London and the rest of the British Isles. Apple Records were quoted as being 'puzzled' by the decision, while United Artists' were said to be both 'annoyed' and 'astonished'. Back-against-the-wall Rank denied that they had suggested that business at the London Pavilion was not as brisk as at first implied. On the question of only screening *Yellow Submarine* in a third of their locations, Rank explained: **"We have played it at 12 theatres outside London. On those results, which had been rather disappointing, a number of theatre bookings for the film have been taken out. This is because the film is obviously not appealing to some people whom one might expect it to."** All this was ammunition enough for sour-faced tabloid writers to dust off their Beatles-are-past-it diatribes.

Three weeks after the *Yellow Submarine* premiere, respected Italian film-maker Federico Fellini announced that he was about to shoot a new movie with an international cast headed by Hollywood legend, 76-year old Mae West, comedians Groucho Marx and Jimmy Durante plus The Beatles who would also be supplying the soundtrack. But the only person who knew about this movie - with a storyline about dissolute times in ancient Rome - seems to have been the director himself. The word from Apple was clear, **"What's he talking about? There have not been any negotiations between them [the Beatles] or Mr Fellini, either about them taking part in the film or writing music for it!"**

YELLOW SUBMARINE

A United Artists Release
King Features Entertainment

Director	George Dunning
Producer	Al Brodax

CAST

John Clive	*voice of John*
Geoffrey Hughes	*voice of Paul*
Paul Angelus	*voice of Ringo & Chief Blue Meani*
Dick Emery	*voice of Lord Mayor & Boob*
Lance Percival	*voice*

CREDITS

Director	George Dunning
Production Company	King Features Entertainment Subafilms, Apple Films, TV Cartoons
Producer	Al Brodax
Associate Producer	Mary Ellen Stewart
Production Supervisor	John Coates
Scriptwriter	Lee Minoff Al Brodax Jack Mendelsohn Erich Segal
Original Story	Lee Minoff
Original Songs	John Lennon Paul McCartney George Harrison
Original Score	George Martin
Cinematography	John Williams
Animation Directors	Jack Stokes & Bob Balser
Animators	Alan Ball Hester Coblentz Rich Cox Arthur Cuthbert Cam Ford Ann Jolliffe Tom Halley Jim Hiltz Arthur Humberstone Reg Lodge Terry Moesker Mike Pocock Edric Radage Mike Stuart
Special Effects Animator	Chris Cannter
Head Checkers	Helen Jones, Margaret Geddes Janet Hosie & Corona Mayer
Background	Alison De Vere
Background	Millie McMillan
Edited	Brian J. Bishop
Designers	Heinz Edelman, John Cramer & Gordon Harrison
Special Effects	Charles Jenkins
Sound	Donald Cohen & Ken Rolls
Length	7830 feet (2387 metres)
Time	87 minutes
UK Premiere	17 July, 1968
US Premiere	13 November, 1968

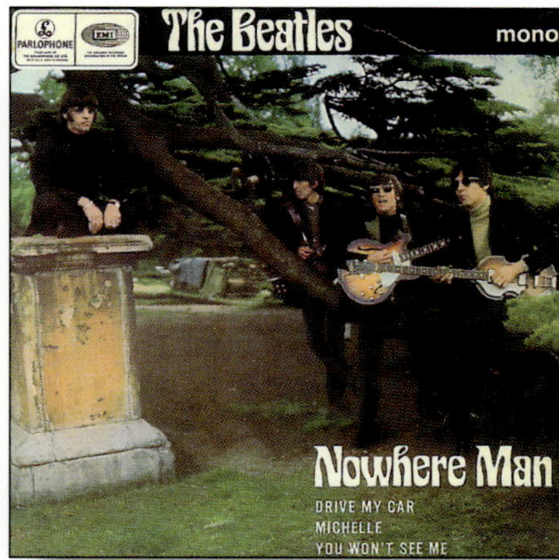

ABOVE FROM LEFT TO RIGHT Swedish version of *'All You Need Is Love'*, Mexican single version of *'Yellow Submarine'* and UK version of *'Nowhere Man'*.

YELLOW SUBMARINE

Apple/Parlophone
PMC 7070 (stereo)
PCS 7070 (stereo)
Produced: George Martin
Released: 17 January, 1969

SIDE ONE

1 **Yellow Submarine** (Ringo)
Thursday, 26 May
Wednesday, 1 June
Thursday, 2 June
Friday 3 June, 1966

2 **Only A Northern Song** (George)
Monday, 13 February
Tuesday, 14 February
Thursday, 20 April
Friday 21 April, 1967

3 **All Together Now** (Paul)
Friday, 12 May, 1967

4 **Hey Bulldog** (John)
only appears in a few prints
Sunday, 11 February, 1968

5 **It's All Too Much** (George)
Thursday, 25 May
Friday, 26 May
Friday, 2 June , 1967
(De Lane Lea Recording Studios)

6 **All You Need Is Love** (John)
Wednesday, 14 June, 1967
(Olympic Studios):
Monday, 19 June
Friday, 23 June
Saturday, 24 June
Sunday 25 June, 1967
(Abbey Road)

SIDE TWO

1 **Pepperland***

2 **Sea Of Time***

3 **Sea Of Holes***

4 **Sea Of Monsters***

5 **March Of The Meanies***

6 **Pepperland Laid Waste***

7 **Yellow Submarine In Pepperland***

(*) Original film score composed and orchestrated by George Martin
Tuesday, 22 October
Wednesday, 23 October, 1968

US VERSION

Apple/Capitol SW153 (stereo)
Released: 13 January, 1969

UK 45s

A: **Eleanor Rigby** (Paul)
B: **Yellow Submarine** (Ringo)
Parlophone R5493
Released: 5 August, 1966

US 45s

A: **Eleanor Rigby**
B: **Yellow Submarine**
Capitol 5715
Released: 8 August, 1966

17

The Films That Never Were: FIVE & SIX

LORD OF THE RINGS & THE THREE MUSKETEERS

In the years when The Beatles were still looking for a big screen follow-up to both *A Hard Day's Night* and *Help!* recurring rumours proliferated of two possible movie ventures: one an adaptation of Tolkein's *Lord Of The Rings* - an epic fairytale which, in the pre-Industrial Light and Magic SFX era, most considered unfilmable, while the second was to be (yet) another high adventure remake of *The Three Musketeers.*

Paul McCartney

'John wanted us to buy the film rights to *Lord Of The Rings*. It was very much his idea. We talked about it for quite a while, but then I started to smell a bit of a carve-up because immediately John wanted to be Bilbo*- wanted the lead and, started to be a bit kinda "ooh, dear wait a minute". But things start to become difficult when somebody has taken the lead without consulting the others and then second lead goes and so you suddenly end up with Zeppo**!'

'The strength of the other films which we made is that we're all equal. I'm not sure what the problem was, but I think that Tolkein's estate who control *Lord Of The Rings* wouldn't sell us the movie rights or maybe they'd already sold them to someone else - so that solved that problem. *The Three Musketeers* came up quite early on...But again, I'm glad that we didn't make either of those two projects, because it would have been quite wildly out of character. I wonder if it had anything to do with the fact that Dick Lester ended up doing both the *Three* and *The Four Musketeers*?'***

What other movie projects were quietly scuppered?

ABOVE In yet another image make-over, the Fabs substitute ruffle collars for the more familiar collarless ones.

Paul McCartney

'Paul Gallico wrote some treatments. There were some interesting ideas put forward, but the trouble was when they actually sent you the script and you read it...it didn't feel like a film...it took more imagination than we had. With those kind of things...when you look at it and it's borderline - that's when you've got to say "no", unless you are a visionary impresario who says, "I believe in this" - then it's not a borderline situation for him. If we didn't believe in something, then that was the signal for all of us to say, "sorry, next please!"'

Setting John and Ringo's solo excursions to one side, as a group The Beatles never stepped out of character in any one of their movies.

'Well, we really only had those two chances to be out of character and the scripts were quite definitely written in character. The rest of the stuff we did as The Beatles was more or less documentary - us playing ourselves. In retrospect, I wouldn't have minded playing a fictitious role...probably quite liked it. The only things I would be quite interested in is not playing myself. I really don't like the idea of playing myself - I did that in *Give My Regards To Broad Street* and I realised afterwards that it

really wasn't much fun trying to play myself. I like the idea of character roles - playing something a million miles from myself. To tell you the truth, these days I'm not that keen. When I was doing *Give My Regards To Broad Street*, I got very...wow, it would be fab-u-lous to do more acting, ...because I really enjoyed the experience, but afterwards I started to think...nah, I don't like what I did too much.'

The Beatles' previous relationship with Richard Lester drove home the truth that it's the director, as much as anyone else, who makes or breaks a film.

Paul McCartney

'When I was doing *Give My Regards To Broad Street* I had this terrible meeting half way through...because we actually took a break half way through the making of it. Anyway, the director broke down and cried...I think he may have been having a bit of a nervous breakdown, but he was crying and I started to think "Oh dear, I'm not sure that this is going to work out" - I should have known then. He was a commercials director and it was one of those things - either it's gonna work bigtime or it won't quite work. And, one or two times when I was talking to him, he didn't like what I was saying and started crying. Maybe, he wanted it right and wanted to please me and when I showed some sort of displeasure...I hate to do that, but my thing has always been trying to get it right. I suppose, I do get a bit obsessive when I'm trying to get things right. And, it can be a little unpleasant for people. But, sometimes, it's necessary to get it right. If you look at a lot of people who get what they're doing right, there's often that ingredient, unfortunately. The alternative, is not to get things right and put up with getting it wrong. And, I think that's kind of what I did on *Broad Street*, really.'

FOOTNOTES:

*** In actual fact, the casting would have been as follows:**

John - *Gollum*

Paul - *Fredo Baggins*

George - *Gandalf*

Ringo - *Sam Merryweather*

****A reference to an earlier member of the Marx Brothers comedy team.**

*****Richard Lester made two sequels to his original 1973 *The Three Musketeers (The Queen's Diamonds)*. They were *The Four Musketeers (The Revenge Of Milady)* (1974) and *The Return Of The Musketeers* (1989).**

ABOVE Every man should have a Hobbit - Young George rehearses as a possible Gandalf.

OPPOSITE PAGE Yoko is not easily bought with a box of chocolates.

18

THE MAGIC CHRISTIAN

Perhaps, only someone as skilled as director Robert Altman can successfully pull off large ensembles features such as his 1975 prototypical production *Nashville.* And, again, later with *The Player.* It's not just a matter of how to best utilise the presence of so many familiar faces (and inflated egos). The secret is to make certain beforehand that the whole endeavour is firmly constructed around a skillfully layered script and a plot with a genuine sense of purpose, rather than ignoring such pre-requisites and just opting to string together a bunch of (often unfunny) in-jokes and sight-gags.

Unfortunately, ego-stroking off-kilter projects such as *Candy* and *The Magic Christian* only succeeded in pandering to the rich, the famous and, the bored shitless acting brigade in pursuit of hipness by virtue of association. Once again, the screenplay was based on a novel by Terry Southern.

Ringo didn't learn from his previous mistake. Though his role was far greater than before - he shared top billing with Peter Sellers - the whole escapade was instantly weighed down by the celebrity baggage that included top line stars such as Richard Attenborough, Laurence Harvey, Christopher Lee, Spike Milligan, Yul Brynner, Roman Polanski, Wilfred Hyde-White, Hattie Jacques, John Le Mesurier, Dennis Price plus Pythonites John Cleese and Graham Chapman (who also supplied additional material to the original script cobbled together by Terry Southern, Peter Sellers and the movie's director, Joe McGrath). On a lighter note, who could ever forget Raquel Welch as a whip wielding scantily clad Amazon disciplining a female crew of topless galley-slaves; infact, it's the only thing about the movie most people can ever recollect!

In the final analysis, even a comic genius such as Peter Sellers could not salvage this celluloid travesty of the world's richest man (Sir Guy Grand) who adopts the down-on-his-luck Ringo (Youngman Grand) and then sets own to demonstrate to him that you can put a price on everyone!

The only good thing to come out of *The Magic Christian* was 'Come And Get It' - a song written and demo'd by Paul McCartney during the 'Abbey Road' sessions and recorded, on 2 August 1969, by Beatle-wannabes, Badfinger (formerly The Iveys).

The single peaked at No.4. The movie sank like a stone.

ABOVE Italian billboard poster for the film.

ABOVE Raquel and Ringo discuss a whip-around for the members of the cast.

RIGHT The soundtrack LP.

THE MAGIC CHRISTIAN

Grand Films

Director Joe McGrath
Producer Denis O'Dell

CAST

Peter Sellers	*Sir Guy Grand*
Ringo Starr	*Youngman Grand*
Richard Attenborough	*Oxford Coach*
Leonard Frey	*Passenger on Ship*
Laurence Harvey	*Hamlet*
Christopher Lee	*Dracula*
Spike Milligan	*Traffic Warden*
Yul Brynner	*Lady Singer*
Roman Polanski	*Man listening to Lady Singer*
Raquel Welch	*Slave-driver*
Isobel Jeans	*Guy's Sister*
Caroline Blakiston	*Guy's Sister*
Wilfred Hyde-White	*Ship's Captain*
Tom Boyle	*My Man Jeff*
Terence Alexander	*Mad Major*
Peter Bayliss	*Pompous Toff*
Joan Benham	*Socialite at Sotheby's*
Patrick Cargill	*Auctioneer*
Graham Chapman	*Oxford Stroke*
John Cleese	*Director in Sotheby's*
Clive Dunn	*Sommerlier*
Freddie Earlle	*Sol*
Fred Emney	*Fitzgibbon*
Kenneth Fortescue	*Irate Snob at Sotheby's*
Peter Graves	*Interested Lord at Ship's Bar*
Patrick Holt	*Duke in Sotheby's*
David Hutcheson	*Lord Barry*
Hattie Jacques	*Ginger Horton*
John Le Mesurier	*Sir John*
Jeremy Lloyd	*Lord Hampton*
David Lodge	*Ship's Guide*
Victor Maddern	*Hot Dog Vendor*
Ferdy Mayne	*Edouard*
Guy Middleton	*Duke of Mantisbriar*
Peter Myers	*Lord Kilgallon*
Dennis Price	*Winthrop*
Robert Raglan	*Maltravers*
Graham Stark	*Waiter*
Leon Thau	*Engine Room Toff*
Frank Thornton	*Police Inspector*
Michael Trubshawe	*Sir Lionel*
Edward Underdown	*Prince Henry*
Michael Aspel	*Television Commentator*
Michael Barrett	*Television Commentator*
Harry Carpenter	*Television Commentator*
W. Barrington Dalby	*Television Commentator*
John Snagge	*Television Commentator*
Alan Whicker	*Television Commentator*

CREDITS

Director	Joe McGrath
Production Company	Grand Films
Producer	Denis O'Dell
Executive Producer	Henry T. Weinstein
	Anthony B. Unger
Production Manager	Victor Peck
Assistant Director	Roger Simons
Scriptwriter	Terry Southern
	Joe McGrath
	Peter Sellers
Additional Material	Graham Chapman
	John Cleese
Original Novel	Terry Southern
Cinematography	Geoffrey Unsworth
Visual Special Effects	Wally Veevers
Cartoon	Richard Williams Studio
Editor	Kevin Connor
Production Designer	Assheton Connor
Art Director	George Djurkovic
Set Director	Peta Button
Music Composer & Conducted	Ken Thorne
Choreography	Lionel Blair
Costumes	Vangie Harrison
Sound Editor	Brian Holland
Sound Recording	Peter Sutton
Sound Re-recording	Gerry Humphreys

Length 8550 feet (2,607 metres)
Time 95 minutes

19

LET IT BE

'*Let It Be* made more money for them than all the others put together. They wanted it for TV, but I told 'em that was stupid.'
Allen Klein

'I think *Let It Be* was good, but it wasn't the film we meant to make. Nevertheless, *Let It Be* is actually a very good film - but, it's a psycho-drama. It's the story of four guys breaking up...it's a horror story for me. Personally? I think it makes for quite a good film.'
Paul McCartney

Having consistently pioneered the kind of recording studio techniques that quickly became everyday currency, by the time they arrived at what was to become *Let It Be*, The Beatles had now gone full circle, finishing up pretty much as they had begun - just three guitars and a drumkit. The controversy that perpetually surrounds *Let It Be*, more often than not concerns itself with the accompanying record album rather than with the actual film. But then, there are those who worked on the movie who claim that it shows only one half of the story, insisting that many of those scenes that ended up on the cutting room floor reveal another mood to the proceedings - one that is lighter, often frivolous and, overall, much less bleak.

Paul McCartney
'I'm sure that's probably quite true, but what it became was the documentary of a break-up...more a *Cathy Come Home* rather than anything else. Those were the most rivetting filmic bits where we were going at each other...and also the sadness of it. I suppose as a director you have to go with that...you just can't start saying, "let's make it pretty."'

The fact that producer Michael Lindsay-Hogg filmed the detailed self-destruction of what many believed to be the quintessential Sixties 'dream' caused great dissent amongst critics and open hostility from fans. So much so, that the Beatles would later return to the studio to record 'Abbey Road' aware that in their misguided attempt to destroy their career and any accompanying myth, an unforgiving public might seek revenge and possibly jeopardise upcoming individual solo projects.

Michael Lindsay-Hogg
'There was material in that film which was the most accurate anywhere about the break-up, showing the kind of ennui they felt. But, because they were the stars as well as the producers, they didn't want that material to be scrutinised by the public. So it came out and part of what I wanted to tell suffered.'

ABOVE Yoko warms up a snack for the lads in the latest state-of-the-art microwave oven.

As with *Magical Mystery Tour*, The Beatles elected to aim this latest film project at television. But this time, there would be no frantic comedy chases, no psychedelic flights of surrealistic fantasy, in fact nothing whatsoever that could possibly alienate a mass audience. For the time being, at least, it would be all singing, all dancing.

The scenario was as basic as they come: The Beatles were going to make a documentary movie about themselves producing a TV show which they would also film. The show itself wasn't going to be an exercise in greatest hits nostalgia and, to this end, they were writing a selection of all-new songs which would later make up their next Apple album.

As with all the best laid plans, things didn't quite pan out the way they had intended! Quite the reverse, the whole thing rapidly fell to pieces along with The Beatles themselves. With a working title of 'Get Back', rehearsals began at Twickenham Studios on 2 January, 1969 and it was sound engineer Glyn Johns' task to record the proceedings. Johns had previously worked with the group on one occasion as an assistant engineer on Jack Good's TV special *Around The Beatles*, but this time around he was in charge of the Big One. Johns would later detail his involvement to noted writer/radio presenter John Tobler during an episode of the BBC Radio One series, *The Record Producers*. The project rapidly ran into trouble. It took just eight days for George Harrison to walk out on the 10th, complaining of continued criticism from McCartney. He returned the following week, however, none of the two weeks of recorded rehearsals were ever officially released, but became the core source of quite probably the most extensive series of bootleg albums ever,

Glyn Johns

'*Let It Be* was something of a fiasco. It proved, however, to be an extraordinarily educational period for me - it obviously couldn't have been anything else, but that was why I wanted to do it, because I knew I'd learn something. The extraordinary thing is that they proved up to that point that they were masters of the 'Produced Record', yet the stuff I did with them wasn't 'produced' in that way at all, it was all recorded live in a rehearsal situation. And for that, I think it has great value, because, for the album, I originally put together an album of rehearsals, with chat and jokes and bits of general conversation in between the tracks, which was the way I wanted *Let It Be* to be - breakdowns, false starts.'

'Really the idea was that, at the time, they were viewed as being the be-all-and-end-all, sort of up there on a pedestal, beyond touch, just gods, completely gods, and what I witnessed going on at these rehearsals was that, in fact, they were hysterically funny, but very ordinary people in many ways and they were capable of playing as a band, which everybody was beginning to wonder about at that point, because they hadn't done so for some time - everything had been prepared in advance, everything had been overdubbed, and they proved in that rehearsal that they could sing and play at the same time, and they could make records without all those weird sounds.'

'That became an obsession with me, and I got the bit between my teeth about it, and one night I mixed a bunch of stuff that they didn't even know I'd recorded half the time - I'd just whacked the recorder on for a lot of stuff that they did, and gave them an acetate the following morning of what I'd done, as a rough idea of what an album could be like, released as it was. There was one thing that only happened once, a song that Paul played to the others, which he later used on one of his ensuing albums, called 'Teddy Boy', and I have a tape of Paul actually teaching the others this song. I loved it, and I was hoping they'd finish it and do it, because I thought it was really good. But my version does go on a bit, and they're just going round and round, trying to get the chord sequence right, I suppose, and the best bit is where John Lennon gets bored - he obviously doesn't want to play it any more, and starts doing his interjections.'

The outcome was that The Beatles didn't feel that the content of the acetate was releasable in its present format so Johns flew to the States to work with the Steve Miller Band. Upon his return to Britain, Johns was summoned to a meeting at EMI at which Lennon and McCartney pointed to a small mountain of tapes. **"Remember that idea you had about putting an album together?...well, there are the tapes - go and do it."** It was definitely panic time for the impressionable young engineer! **"I was absolutely petrified. I was actually being asked to put together a Beatles album on my own."**

RIGHT The soundtrack LP.

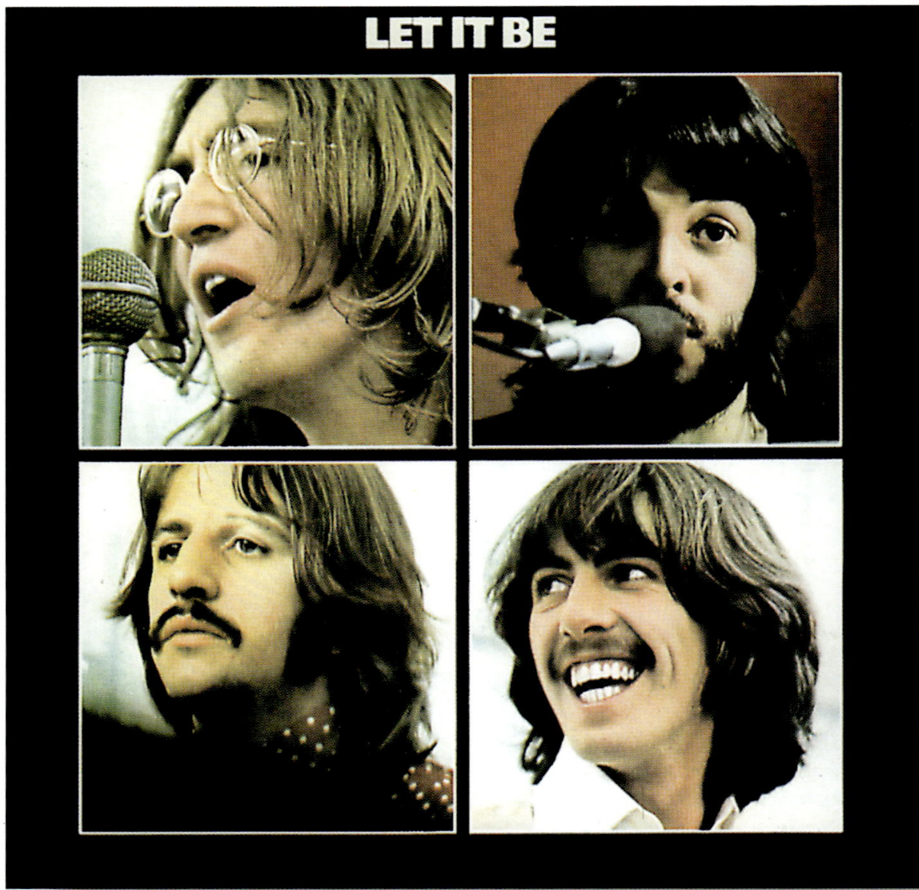

John Lennon
'We didn't want to know. It's the first time since the first album that we didn't have anything to do with it.'

So, six weeks after the end of the 'Get Back' sessions, Glyn Johns - who by now was also involved in the recording of 'Abbey Road' - entered Olympic Sound Studios (10 March) to embark upon the task of selecting and editing an album's worth of acceptable material from over thirty hours of tapes. On the first day, Johns extracted eleven tracks.

1 **Get Back**
(Tuesday, 28 January)
2 **Teddy Boy**
(Friday, 24 January)
3 **On Our Way Home (Two Of Us)**
(Friday, 24 January)
4 **Dig A Pony**
(Wednesday, 22 January)
5 **I Got A Feeling**
(Wednesday, 22 January)
6 **The Long And Winding Road**
(Friday, 31 January)
7 **Let It Be**
(Friday, 31 January)
8 **The Rocker**
(Wednesday, 22 January)
9 **Save The Last Dance For Me**
(Wednesday, 22 January)
10 **Don't Let Me Down**
(Wednesday, 22 January)
9 **Because You're Sweet And Lovely (For You Blue)**
(Saturday, 25 January)
10 **Get Back**
(Tuesday, 28 January)
11 **The Walk**
(Monday, 27 January)

On 13 March, 1969, Johns turned his attention to piecing together a medley of impromptu rock 'n' R&B covers.

1 **Maggie May**
(Friday, 24 January)

2 **Rock 'n' Roll Medley:**
Shake Rattle And Roll / Kansas City / Miss Ann / Lawdy Miss Clawdy / Blue Suede Shoes / You Really Got A Hold On Me
(Sunday, 26 January)

After much consideration Johns completed his suggestion for the album of the 'Get Back' project on 28 May, 1969, with a revised track listing.

Side One

1 **The One After 909**
(Thursday, 30 January)

2 **Rocker**
(Wednesday, 22 January)

3 **Save The Last Dance For Me**
(Wednesday, 22 January)

4 **Don't Let Me Down**
(Wednesday, 22 January)

5 **Dig A Pony**
(Friday, 24 January)

6 **I've Got A Feeling**
(Friday, 24 January)

7 **Get Back** - single version
(Tuesday, 28 January)

Side Two

1 **For You Blue**
(Saturday, 25 January)

2 **Teddy Boy**
(Friday, 24 January)

3 **Two Of Us**
(Friday, 24 January)

4 **Maggie May**
(Friday, 24 January)

5 **Dig It**
(Sunday, 26 January)

6 **Let It Be**
(Friday, 31 January
& Wednesday, 30 April)

7 **The Long and Winding Road**
(Friday, 31 January)

8 **Get Back - reprise**
(Tuesday, 28 January)

Six years down the line, photographer Angus McBean's good-natured recreation of the Fabs' 1963 debut album - which again depicted them on the main staircase of the EMI building - had been approved with the whole package titled 'Get Back' with 'Let It Be' and 11 other songs. At the time, Johns was given to understand that his work had been approved and was just waiting to go into production. However, this was a time continually fraught with indecision, paranoia and, frequently, poor judgement. Johns, who takes credit for the legendary performance that took place high up on the roof of the Apple HQ in Savile Row, on 30 January, was witness to many of these dramas.

Glyn Johns
'The TV show had been shelved, because they couldn't find anywhere to do it - Paul wanted it to be like a barn dance sort of thing originally. Then, they wanted to do something with a lot of their fans there, and

they wanted to do it outside, but since it was during the winter months, we couldn't really do it in a park or anything like that. Then they thought about hiring an ocean liner and putting all the fans on it, playing for them on the way to wherever we were going, some island with an open amphitheatre where they could play to the fans again, then put them all back on the liner and go home again.'

Along with a number of other exotic suggestions, such ideas were soon abandoned. Johns then suggested recording a selection of their new songs in the controlled atmosphere of a studio. **"Since there was already a documentary about the songs being written and rehearsed, if a film was made of them recording, playing the songs properly, it would provide an end to the film."** The Beatles approved the idea and elected to record in their newly constructed studio in the basement of the Apple building. But, according to Johns, it was a total disaster area, so he quickly borrowed some mobile equipment from EMI which was used to do the recording.

There was still the unresolved problem of how they could play to infinitely more people than could be accommodated in a studio where they were recording. At the time, plans were being made to transform the rooftop area of the Apple Corp HQ into a tranquil roof garden. One lunchtime, Johns, Michael Lindsay-Hogg and Ringo decided to inspect the proposed site of such renovation.

Glyn Johns
'Sure enough, you could play to the whole of London from up there - we thought. So they set it up, and it worked well...my version of the album actually starts with 'One After 909', which was recorded on the roof.'

What was to be The Beatles' last ever public performance took place around lunchtime, on Thursday, 30 January, and lasted all of 42 minutes. In probability, it would have carried on indefinitely had it not been for the neighbours. Following up on a number of public complaints, the police abruptly brought things to a close which prompted McCartney to utter, **"You've been playing on the roofs again, and you know your Momma doesn't like it, she's gonna have you arrested."** But it's Lennon who gets in the final word with, **"I'd like to say 'thank you' on behalf of the group and ourselves and I hope we passed the audition!"**

Apple's next-door neighbour, woollen merchant Stanley Davis, was obviously not a Beatles' fan, **"I want this bloody noise stopped. It's an absolute disgrace,"** he huffed. Neither too was Stephen King, the chief accountant at the nearby Royal Bank of Scotland who freely admitted putting through a call to the Boys In Blue. However, another Savile Row banker, Alan Pulverness, was of a friendlier disposition: **"Some people just can't appreciate good music."**

ABOVE 20th anniversary picture disc version of 'Hey Jude'.

Up until then, The Beatles - with the addition of Billy Preston on electric piano - had swaggered through three takes of 'Get Back', two each of 'Don't Let Me Down' and 'I've Got A Feeling' plus singles takes of 'The One After 909', 'Dig A Pony' plus an impromptu 'God Save The Queen' while tapes were being changed over, in the following order:

Get Back
Get Back
Don't Let Me Down
I've Got A Feeling
The One After 909
Dig A Pony
God Save The Queen
I've Got A Feeling
Don't Let Me Down
Get Back

His first attempt at putting together the 'Get Back' album having been shelved, Glyn Johns was then asked to reassemble a new album but, this time, one that would reflect the movie. By 5 January, 1970, he had come up with a suitably revised version.

Side One

1 **The One After 909**
(Thursday, 30 January)

2 **Rocker**
(Wednesday, 22 January)

3 **Save The Last Dance For Me**
(Wednesday, 22 January)

4 **Don't Let Me Down**
(Wednesday, 22 January)

5 **Dig A Pony**
(Friday, 24 January)

6 **I've Got A Feeling**
(Friday, 24 January)

7 **Get Back** - single version
(Tuesday, 28 January)

8 **Let It Be**
(Friday, 31 January
& Wednesday, 30 April)

Side Two

1 **For You Blue**
(Saturday, 25 January)

2 **Two Of Us**
(Friday, 24 January)

3 **Maggie May**
(Friday, 24 January)

4 **Dig It**
(Sunday, 26 January

5 **The Long and Winding Road**
(Friday, 31 January)

6 **I Me Mine**
(Saturday, 3 January, 1970)

7 **Across The Universe**
(Sunday, 4 February
& Thursday, 8 February 1968)

8 **Get Back**
(Tuesday, 28 January)

Things appear to have been left in limbo until 23 March. On that date, a new player entered the arena, when American producer Phil Spector arrived at Abbey Road faced with the daunting task of extracting an album from the same tape cache that Glyn Johns had previous researched. If any one record maker justifies 'legendary' status, then it surely must be Phil Spector who, following a two-year period of self-exile after the Stateside flop of 'River Deep, Mountain High' by Ike and Tina Turner, was back in business, though somewhat more subdued. With an ego to match his Wagnerian kitchen-

ABOVE Rockin' on the rooftop of the Apple HQ. With this being on Savile Row, suits are the order of the day.

sink-and-all productions, 'River Deep, Mountain High' was Spector's most spectacular creation to date, and a record regarded by many as one of the greatest ever fashioned.

For all manner of reasons (some professional, some personal), it may have failed in its country of origin, but in Britain the scenario was reversed. Decca promotions' man Tony Hall proved himself to be the pivotal force that rallied radio (both land-based legit and off-shore pirate) behind 'River Deep, Mountain High' and chased it up to Number 2 on the nation's charts.

Previous to this, Phil Spector was the music industry's first self-made teenage millionaire, the creator of the unique echo-drenched wide-screen 'Wall Of Sound' which he had employed to great effect on dozens of classic pop singles including 'Da Doo Ron Ron' (The Crystals), 'Be My Baby' (The Ronettes), 'You've Lost That Lovin' Feelin' (The Righteous Brothers) all of which he had released on his own Philles label.

This time around, Spector resurfaced, not on the resurrected Philles label, but on A&M Records - a successful Los Angeles enterprise, jointly run by Tijuana Brass star Herb Alpert and his long-time sidekick Jerry Moss and, home to The Carpenters. However, the familiar A&M logo shared label space with the title 'Phil Spector Productions' accompanied by a caricature of a small (somewhat sinister) figure in top hat and cloak. Spector's new roster of talent was headed by The Ronettes (featuring the Voice of Veronica) and The Checkmates Ltd, whose single 'Black Pearl' had lodged at Number 13 on the US Hot 100. Also released, for the first time in the States, on this new enterprise, was the 'River Deep, Mountain High' LP .

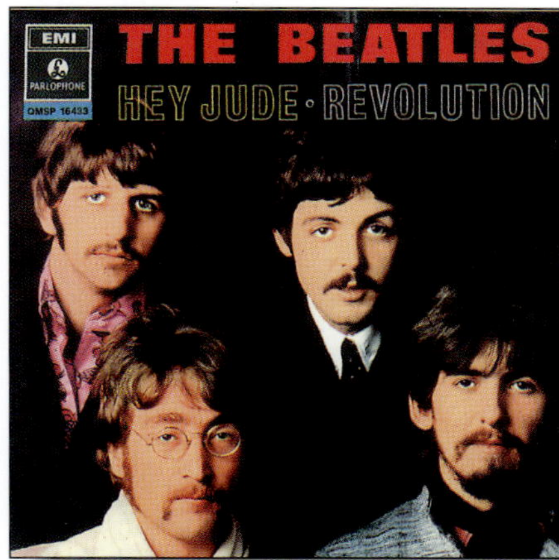

ABOVE Spanish version of the single *'Hey Jude'.*

There were two strap-lines on the sleeve. The first said, 'An Historic Recording by Phil Spector', while the second proclaimed: 'River Deep, Mountain High' is a perfect record from start to finish. You couldn't improve on it' - and was signed George Harrison.

Spector and The Beatles might have been friends from way back (The Ronettes were among the support acts on the group's final US concert tour) but it was Allen Klein who reintroduced the respective parties to one another on a business level. Before this, The Beatles had ruminated that if they ever needed a producer other than George Martin, it would be Spector. Similarly, Spector made no secret that he had always wanted to work with the lovable mop-tops.

Despite unprecedented international success, British recording artists didn't disguise their unshakable belief that American studios (and their engineers) were infinitely superior to their UK equivalents - this theory was based primarily on the unique sounds exclusive to such labels as Motown, Specialty, Stax and Sun plus anything whiz kid Spector had laid his hands on, but, as Lennon insisted, **"It was usually the man, not the studio."** In this instance, that man was Phil Spector. As a result of Klein's intervention, Spector came away with two commissions; the first, to salvage the 'Get Back' tapes somehow and secondly, to record a Lennon/Plastic Ono Band single ('Instant Karma'). "**He did a great job,"** John Lennon later said of Spector's controversial studio make-over. **"He took the shittiest load of badly recorded shit with a lousy feeling to it ever, and he made something of it."**

Up until Spector's involvement, Lennon thought it would be productive to release the 'shitty' version, because 'it would break up The Beatles...it would break the myth.' **"I thought it was good to let it out and show people what had happened to us, this is where we're at now, we can't get it together, we don't play together anymore...leave us alone. I was stoned all the time and didn't give a shit about nothin'...and nobody else did."**

With George Harrison and Allen Klein on hand for most of the time, Spector spent the Monday, 23 March working on 'I've Got A Feeling', 'Dig A Pony', 'The One After 909', 'I Me Mine' and 'Across The Universe'. Two days later, (25 March), Spector turned his attention to 'For You Blue', 'Teddy Boy' and 'Two Of Us.' The following day Spector called up the tapes for 'The Long And Winding Road', 'Let it Be', 'Get Back' and 'Maggie May'. Come Friday (27 March), 'Dig It' was the only music track worked on, the remainder of the day being devoted to chopping up sections of miscellaneous studio dialogue.

On Monday (30 March), Spector tape-lopped a 16-second instrumental sound-byte he'd cut from 'For You Blue' and overdubbed it with all manner of incidental sounds and dialogue from the movie. It never made the final short-list but then, neither did the instrumental 'Rocker', a cover of the Drifters' 'Save The Last Dance For Me' or 'Teddy Boy' - the latter being re-recorded by McCartney for his solo debut. All Fools Day (1 April) and Spector marched 36 musicians and a 14-piece choir (under Richard Hewson's direction) into Abbey Road's Studio One where, drenched in his familiar Cathedral-like echo, Phil Spector overdubbed 'Across The Universe', 'The Long And Winding Road' and 'I Me Mine'. One more spot of studio time (2 April) had Spector mixing the previous day's work and tidying up any loose ends. After what had seemed like an eternity, the 'Get Back' project - now renamed 'Let It Be' - was at long last finished, then subsequently programmed and prepared for a 8 May, 1970 release:

ABOVE UK export version of *'Hey Jude'.*

Side One

1 **Two Of Us** (Paul)
Friday, 31 January, 1969
(Apple Studios)

2 **Dig A Pony** (John)
Thursday, 30 January, 1969
(Apple Corp rooftop)

3 **Across The Universe** (John)
Sunday, 4 February
& Thursday, 8 February, 1968
(Abbey Road)

4 **I Me Mine** (George)
Saturday, 3 January, 1970
(Abbey Road)

5 **Dig It** (John)
Friday, 24 January
& Sunday, 26 January, 1969
(Apple Studios)

6 **Let It Be** (Paul)
Saturday, 25 January
& Wednesday, 30 April, 1969
(Abbey Road)

7 **Maggie May** (38 second snippet)
Friday, 24 January, 1969
(Apple Studios)

Side Two

1 **I've Got A Feeling** (Paul)
Thursday, 30 January, 1969
(Apple Corp rooftop)

2 **The One After 909** (John/Paul)
Thursday, 30 January, 1969
(Apple Corp rooftop)

3 **The Long And Winding Road** (Paul)
Friday, 31 January, 1969
(Apple Studios);
Wednesday, 1 April, 1970
(Abbey Road)

4 **For You Blue** (George)
Saturday, 25 January, 1969
(Apple Studios)

5 **Get Back** (Paul)
Monday, 27 January, 1969
(Apple Studios);
Thursday, 30 January, 1969
(Apple Corp rooftop)

George Martin's production of 'Let It Be' had been released on 6 March 1970 as a single without too much adverse comment on the production whereas, in contrast, the album of the same name was greeted with critical hostility when it eventually went on sale on 8 May, 1970. Under a heading that proclaimed 'New LP Shows They Couldn't Care Less', Alan Smith, writing for New Musical Express, didn't pull any punches: **"If the new Beatles' soundtrack album 'Let It Be' is to be their last then it will stand as a cheapskate epitaph, a cardboard tombstone, a sad and tatty end to a musical fusion which wiped clean and drew again the face of pop music."** Even the fact that the album came housed in a slip case that included a book of 250 glossy photographs taken on the set didn't appease Smith who was previously regarded as one of the group's most high-profile supporters.

Spector admitted that for him, the 'Get Back' project proved an even greater disaster than the last days of Philles. Suddenly, being branded as the person who 'ruined The Beatles', caused him further distress. But the fact remained, The Beatles hadn't wanted the tracks released in their original state. They said to Spector: **"You can be the judge of it, if you like it, because we're really not involved in it and don't like it any more."** That wasn't good enough for Phil Spector who insisted that they be the final judges. And, according to Spector, they sent him a telegram stating: **"It's great, this is okay, you're taking a great burden off us all."** But, in no way did this resolve many outstanding grievances associated with this ill-starred project.

Police stop Beatles 'making a din'

RAY CONNOLLY

Police stopped the Beatles from filming on the roof of the Apple offices in Savile Row today after getting dozens of complaints about the noise.

The noise of amplified guitars and reverberating voices infuriated some businessmen.

Company director Mr. Stanley Davis, a next-door neighbour of Apple, said: "I want this bloody noise stopped. It's an absolute disgrace.

"You can't even use your telephones, dictate a letter or have your windows open."

The Beatles were filming a television spectacular, which is being built around a new long-playing record.

But the noise—even of the Beatles' noise—was too much for some people.

A police spokesman said: "We had so many complaints we sent someone round. A tremendous din was being made."

The new-look Paul McCartney,

Hundreds of people thronged Savile Row and adjoining Burlington Gardens and looked up at the roof where about a dozen people could be seen taking part in the recording.

Office girls hung out of windows to listen to the Beatles singing.

"Don't let me down," boomed the voice of Paul McCartney. And "I am to miss the train."

After the police arrived the session came to a halt—despite the groans of hundreds of fans who were enjoying the unexpected show.

"Everyone on the balconies and the roof seemed to be enjoying the session," said Mr. Alan Pulverness, who works in a nearby bank. "Some people just can't appreciate good music."

A spokesman for Apple said: "It was all supposed to be very hush-hush. But when you put the Beatles on top of a building in the middle of London and ask them to sing a song it is rather difficult to keep it secret."

Raising the roof—The Beatles during their performance for a film sequence on the roof of Apple's Savile Row offices today—before the police called.

With the Beatles here is the film's director Michael Lindsay-Hogg standing next to John Lennon's friend Yoko Ono.

Four portraits of 'Let It Be' Beatles

NEW LP SHOWS THEY COULDN'T CARE LESS

Have Beatles sold out? asks NME's Alan Smith

IF the new Beatles soundtrack album "Let It Be" is to be their last then it will stand as a cheapskate epitaph, a cardboard tombstone a sad and tatty end to a musical fusion which wiped clean and drew again the face of pop music. At £3—bar a penny—can this mini-collection of new tracks, narcissistic pin-ups and chocolate box dressing really be the last will and testament of the once-respected and most-famous group in the world?

What kind of contempt for the intelligence of today's record-buyer is it that foists upon them an album at this price with seven new tracks; two bits of dressing in the shape of "Dig It" and "Magie May"; and the three previously-released numbers "Let It Be," "Get Back" and "Across The Universe."?

I suspect, in fact, that almost £1 of the cost is to cover the accompanying book of fab glossy pix . . . and lump it or leave it, music lovers.

ON THE RECKONING OF THIS ALBUM THE BEATLES HAVE IN ANY EVENT LOST THEIR SELF-RESPECT AND SOLD OUT ALL THE PRINCIPLES FOR WHICH THEY EVER STOOD.

Remember all those quotes about "the men in suits," and the contempt for candyfloss Hollywood chorales, and the earnest pride in their albums, and the fervent yearning to reject phoneyness right along the line? Forget it . . . because with this LP, the philosophy seems to be exactly one of hype in a pretty packet.

The Beatles are, or were, about music — not the waffle surrounding and enclosed with "Let It Be." And it pains me to see them go along, or accept, this load of old flannel and musical castration.

THE TRAGEDY IS THAT WHAT LITTLE REMAINS OF THE ORIGINAL ALBUM (THIS SET TIES IN WITH THE SOUNDTRACK OF THE DOCUMENTARY FILM "LET IT BE") IS SOME OF THE BEST STRAIGHT ROCK THE BEATLES HAVE RECORDED IN YEARS.

Almost all of the fun and raw feel has been taken away or polished up by Phil Spector, who was called in by Allen Klein to give a nice professional "re-production" to the LP, but he does leave in Lennon's intro to the opener "Two of Us."

"'I Dig A Pygmy' by Charles Hawtrey and the Deaf Aids," bawls Lennon. "Phase One, in which Doris gets her oats."

Doris' oats turn out to be a kind of honey-soft rocker about going home, sung by McCartney with, I think, Lennon harmonising. And if McCartney and Lennon ever get dark days of nostalgia about their past, then this is the one for the record-player.

Next is the short Lennon "Dig A Pony" ("you can penetrate any place you go,"); then Lennon's ethereal and beautiful "Across The Universe," in which he sings that "nothing's gonna change my world."

Following track is George's Russian-flavoured "I Me Mine," a strong ballad with a frantic centre; then it's Lennon's "Can You Dig It," which is no more than a few seconds' of a smile-raising chant about a number of items from the FBI to Matt Busby; then McCartney with a version of "Let It Be" and then another few seconds of the old Liverpool balla of "Maggie May."

SIDE TWO starts with a good McCartney rocker, "I've Got A Feeling with cymbals, screams and Lennon coming in with a hushed-voice refra about "having a good time and putting the floor down." Both this and t follower, "One After 909," are excellent stuff in which McCartney a Lennon really work together.

Next is a predictably beautiful ballad from McCartney, "The Long a Winding Road" — and I can understand why he should object to t heavenly choir and other trimmings which were added without his permissio

In its original form, this song had empty simplicity. Now it's all obtrusi Mantovani-type strings and Cinemascope chorale . . . acceptable . . . b totally unnecessary.

The worst development in the fortunes of the Beatles is that where their finances may be one thing, interference in their individual wo without their control — as in "Long and Winding Road" — is somethi else altogether.

Final tracks are another strong one from George, a whispery chun rocker called "For You Blue" ("Elmore James," he calls out at one poi "got nothin' on this baby!"); and then "Get Back."

THE WORST THING ABOUT THE EXCELLENT LIVE NUMBERS ON TH ALBUM IS THAT THERE ARE SO FEW OF THEM. THE NEXT WORST THIN IS THAT THEY ARE DRESSED UP IN AN ABUNDANCE OF GLOSSY CA AND PAPER AND PUSHED OUT AT £3 MINUS ONE PENNY.

The tragedy is that on the strength of the little new music there is on th LP, the Beatles were never informally better, never more with their fe on the ground.

George Harrison believes the Beatles will work together again and, if o to restore the respect of those who admire appreciate and love them, pray that he is right.

I have followed, vaunted and glowed with Merseyside pride at t achievements of the Beatles since the pre-"Love Me Do" days of t Blue Angel and New Brighton Tower.

But in its overwrapped state, this glorified EP is a bad and sad mistake

It's not surprising that Glyn Johns was less than complementary when the subject of Spector's involvement became the topic of discussion:

> 'I cannot bring myself to listen to the Phil Spector version of the album - I heard a few bars of it once, and was totally disgusted...I think it's an absolute load of garbage!'

He makes no attempt to disguise his bias towards Spector's work being used in preference to his:

> 'It upset me. I wouldn't have minded so much if things hadn't happened in the way they did. First of all, after the Beatles broke up, John Lennon, as an individual, took the tapes and gave them to Phil Spector without the others even being aware of it, which was extraordinary. I think Spector did the most atrocious job, just utter puke...mind you the film's even worse - it was atrocious. I was there when it was being shot, and there was some amazing stuff - their humour got to me as much as the music, and I didn't stop laughing for six weeks. John Lennon only had to walk in a room and I'd just crack up. Their whole mood was wonderful that was the thing, and there was all this nonsense going on at the time about the problems surrounding the group, and the Press being at them. In fact, there they were, just doing it, having a wonderful time and being incredibly funny, and none of that's in the film.'

Johns attributed this to Allen Klein who became the group's manager after all the footage had been shot.

> 'Klein saw a rough cut of it and said he didn't want anyone else in the film but The Beatles, so everyone else who was in any shot at any time was taken out, the net result being that it got a bit difficult to watch after a while.'

Amongst the material left on the cutting room floor were scenes involving various members of the crew and visitors such as Billy Preston.

> 'So what was originally going on was a rehearsal, and there was an interchange, and you saw how things happened, you saw a song grow, and you saw conversations between people - that was all taken out, and hence it was ruined. And then, of course, the Spector thing ruined the record as well, so everyone might as well not bothered.'

Yet, for all the criticism and flak that ensued the *Let It Be* album grabbed a Grammy. A quarter of a century on, those close to the event still continue to carp whenever the complex details surrounding the album and Spector's so-called 'salvage' operation are debated.

> **Paul McCartney**
> 'And I'm one of them. See, it was all done over my head. I had an acetate of the final mixes that Glyn Johns had done and I remember taking it home and listening to it with him and thinking, shit this is like 'wow' - now, today, it would sound like unplugged because it was very basic...very bare...I got a very white feeling...a very bare feeling off it...and I thought, "fuck, this is good...really good, we're reduced to just bare bones...there's something great about it...something very compelling." But Allen Klein stuck his oar in and the others were besotted with him at the time, because he was a very good talker and he said, "Look, I don't think it's right", and he made a lot of decisions. I think it was his decision to bring Phil in.'

Time may have partly healed old scars, but at the time of The Beatles' breakup, McCartney cited Spector's (unwanted) involvement as just one of the reasons he wanted out.

> 'Now, I don't blame Phil...I don't think they've ruined it, but I would have preferred the original bare album. But around that time it was beginning to escape all of us - John was really more interested in Yoko...we were all sort of feeling that we had come to the end of ...not so much our tether, but our pieces of string...the little bunny rabbits' batteries were running down...we were all very fraught with each other and just about everything else. We were probably all on the verge of nervous breakdowns.'

ABOVE And they all lived happily ever after.

Nevertheless, even to consider releasing Glyn Johns' version of the 'Get Back' tapes to accompany the movie was a brave stance to adopt when the public were accustomed to such rich sounding Beatles' records as 'Sgt Pepper' and 'The White Album.'

Paul McCartney

'I think that *Let It Be* is a good film for that reason alone. Sure, it was painful for me at the time, but I couldn't deny that it made for a good film...but it was a really painful film to make and to watch and to think, "oh fuck, here I am arguing with my best friend". Painful it may be but it was good for the film. By then I'm not sure if anyone was approving anything - we just thought, yeah, let it go out the way it is. I think we were all just crazed with each other by then. Though, I remember picking up an Oscar for it off John Wayne - Big Leggy, for the best music score.'

But, as Lennon insisted, nobody was genuinely interested in making the movie as the tension on the Twickenham sound stage increased, **"We'd be there at eight in the morning and you couldn't make music at eight in the mornin' or any other time for that matter."**

Depending upon what narcotic cocktail he was imbibing or who he was hanging out with, Lennon's regard towards The Beatles varied greatly in later years. To this author, Lennon waxed warmly about how he regarded The Beatles only as the group that played around Liverpool and Hamburg before being 'runover by fuckin' Beatlemania or whatever you want to call it.' He had a fondness for watching the Beatles' cartoon series on TV and *A Hard Day's Night* and *Help!* whenever they were screened. However, to others he could be quite vitriolic, paranoid, conspiratorial, particularly on the subject of *Let It Be*.

John Lennon

'I felt sad. That film was set up by Paul. That's one of the main reasons The Beatles ended; I can't speak for George, but I pretty damn well know - we got fed up being sidemen for Paul. The camera work was set up to show Paul and not to show anybody else. And that's how I felt about it. As for the album? I'm fucked if I know. But, one of those versions that was put together when it was still 'Get Back' was pretty damn good. It was the one that turned up as a bootleg and I got the blame. People reckon I was responsible for it. Maybe I was. Can't remember! They said it came from an acetate that I gave to someone who then went and broadcast it as being an advance pressing or something. If that's true, then I suppose I am responsible. But, it's not as though I was pressing them up and selling them out the back door!'

Nevertheless, of the dozen recordings which constituted the 'official' album, two of them 'Get Back' and the title track, were Johns' work of which he is justifiably proud despite the fact that he wasn't afforded any production credit. Johns is convinced that had his original version been released, as opposed to Spector's incarnation, then he would have been offered the same production credit that has appeared on some of the bootleg editions.

'Lennon was the only one who questioned it - I sat each of them down, and said, "Look, I know you originally employed me to be engineer on these sessions, but I consider that as there was no producer, and as I was the only one there and I've actually put it together on my own, I'd really appreciate a producer's credit. I don't want any royalties or any money, just a credit."'

Paul, George and Ringo felt that his request was not unreasonable, but John couldn't understand why Johns wasn't after additional financial remuneration. Johns painstakingly explained to Lennon that it didn't matter who produced the sessions, The Beatles would still sell 'three billion zillion records', adding, **"so I didn't deserve a royalty on their records, but obviously, if my name was there as producer, and I was only asking for a credit for what I'd done, then clearly I would benefit from it in other ways, and it would assist my career, to say the least. I think John finally understood, and anyway, my version of the album never did come out, so there was nothing in contention anyway."**

If there was displeasure concerning the outcome of *Let It Be*, John, George and Ringo didn't reveal it, for Phil Spector was appointed Apple's A&R director going on to produce 'All Things Must Pass' (George Harrison) and 'John Lennon/Plastic Ono Band' and thereafter 'Imagine' (John Lennon) and 'Concert For Bangla Desh' (George Harrison) and, finally two more Lennon projects, 'Sometime In New York City' and 'Rock 'n' Roll'.

On July 1, 1969 work commenced on 'Abbey Road' which was recorded, mixed and in the stores while 'Let It Be' (still referred to as 'Get Back') was being laboured over and still ten months away from release.

December 1970: And, in another universe, the four members of the world's most popular prefab four - The Rutles experienced the same personal dilemmas. As a result, Dirk sued Stig and Nasty, Barry sued Dirk, Nasty sued Stig and Barry and Stig sued himself accidentally. It was the end of a golden era, and the beginning of another one, for lawyers everywhere.

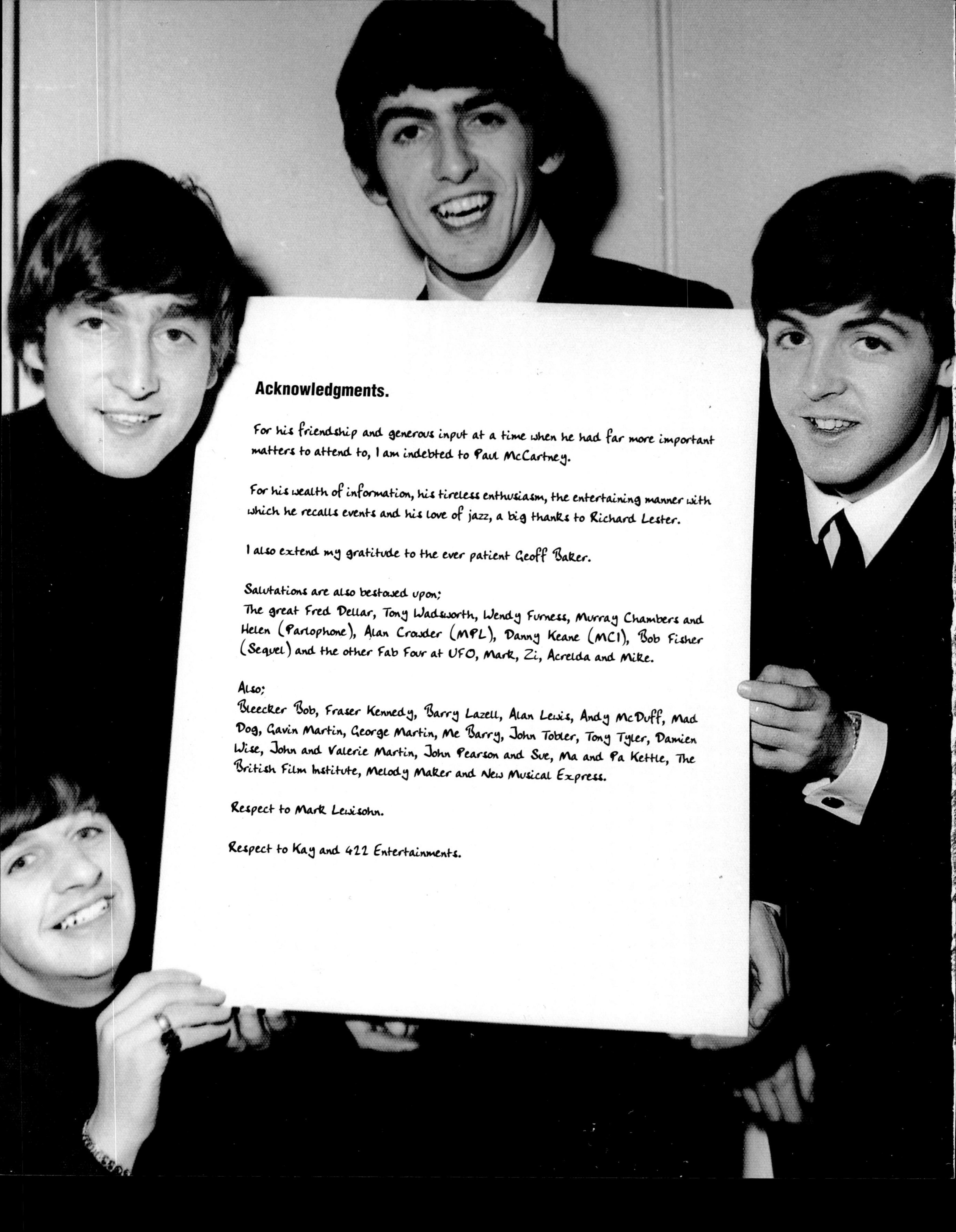

Acknowledgments.

For his friendship and generous input at a time when he had far more important matters to attend to, I am indebted to Paul McCartney.

For his wealth of information, his tireless enthusiasm, the entertaining manner with which he recalls events and his love of jazz, a big thanks to Richard Lester.

I also extend my gratitude to the ever patient Geoff Baker.

Salutations are also bestowed upon;
The great Fred Dellar, Tony Wadsworth, Wendy Furness, Murray Chambers and Helen (Parlophone), Alan Crowder (MPL), Danny Keane (MCI), Bob Fisher (Sequel) and the other Fab Four at UFO, Mark, Zi, Acrelda and Mike.

Also;
Bleecker Bob, Fraser Kennedy, Barry Lazell, Alan Lewis, Andy McDuff, Mad Dog, Gavin Martin, George Martin, Me Barry, John Tobler, Tony Tyler, Damien Wise, John and Valerie Martin, John Pearson and Sue, Ma and Pa Kettle, The British Film Institute, Melody Maker and New Musical Express.

Respect to Mark Lewisohn.

Respect to Kay and 422 Entertainments.